BUSINESS SIMULATED

PRAISE FOR *BUSINESS SIMULATED*

The challenges brought about by rapid technological change and troubling events such as COVID-19 make good strategic leadership more important than ever.

In this book, Michael provides a brilliant, practical and insightful approach to how you can help your people develop the strategic leadership skills needed to be fit for the future.

STEPHAN VON SCHUCKMANN,
MEMBER OF THE BOARD OF MANAGEMENT, ZF GROUP

Michael shares the art of business simulations that translate real-world challenges into engaging learning experiences. A practical handbook for anyone seeking to build capability by testing business leaders and decision-making in context.

ANITA FLEMING, CO-FOUNDER & DIRECTOR AT FOURFOLD CONSULTING

Simulating the future before it happens is simply good business. This book is the business equivalent to Einstein's thought experiments.

MATT CHURCH, FOUNDER OF THOUGHT LEADERS,
AUTHOR OF *RISE UP: AN EVOLUTION IN LEADERSHIP*

They say timing is everything and this book has been gifted to business leaders, entrepreneurs and CEOs at a time when it is most needed.

A CEO's job is to deliver predictability, therefore, rather than leave success to chance, this book offers a solution to test it.

To be better prepared for crisis, uncertainty and ongoing change, those businesses who thrive have created a culture of employees with an ownership mindset, who are practised in responding to business challenges.

This book not only reveals why business simulation is a clever methodology for building muscle in employees' decision making, but also offers a practical solution to creating learning environments for employees that are experiential, fun and lead teams to be actively engaged in the business strategy.

JAQUIE SCAMMELL, AUSTRALIA'S LEADING EXPERT ON CUSTOMER SERVICE

Business simulations are one of the most effective ways for organisations to build capability and accelerate strategy execution. Michael, a master at the craft of business simulations, provides a compelling case and clear framework for embedding simulations as a learning technology and strategy accelerator in your organisation. If you want your people to be more empowered to make good decisions in fast-changing and complex environments, Michael shows you how to do it through business simulations.

GERHARD DIEDERICKS, PARTNER AT KINCENTRIC

A close friend and former colleague, Michael is a master at conceptualising, designing and facilitating strategy simulations. In this book, he shares more than fifteen years of brilliant first-hand insight and experience as to why, how and what makes this learning methodology so effective. It is a must-read for any business wanting to step-change the effectiveness of their leaders and organisation.

CARLO RISI, VP AT STRATEGY INDUSTRYMASTERS

Published by Grammar Factory Publishing, an imprint of MacMillan Company Limited.

Grammar Factory Publishing
MacMillan Company Limited
25 Telegram Mews, 39th Floor, Suite 3906
Toronto, Ontario, Canada
M5V 3Z1

www.grammarfactory.com

Schlosser, Michael–
Business Simulated: Stop Guessing, Start Testing /MichaelSchlosser.

Paperback ISBN 978-1-989737-29-3
eBook ISBN 978-1-989737-30-9

1.BUS019000 BUSINESS & ECONOMICS / Decision-Making & Problem Solving.
2. BUS000000 BUSINESS & ECONOMICS / General. 3. BUSINESS & ECONOMICS / Management Science.

Production Credits
Printed in Australia by IngramSpark
Cover design by Designerbility
Interior layout design by Dania Zafar
Book production and editorial services by Grammar Factory Publishing

Grammar Factory's Carbon Neutral Publishing Commitment
From January 1st, 2020 onwards, Grammar Factory Publishing is proud to be neutralizing the carbon footprint of all printed copies of its authors' books printed by or ordered directly through Grammar Factory or its affiliated companies through the purchase of Gold Standard-Certified International Offsets.

Disclaimer

BUSINESS SIMULATED

STOP GUESSING, START TESTING

MICHAEL SCHLOSSER

CONTENTS

INTRODUCTION

THE ENERGY IN THE ROOM WAS ELECTRIC. THEY WERE SITTING on the edge of their seats, waiting for the final reveal. Had they won? Had they outperformed their peers? Click! The final slide appeared, and they were up on their feet, cheering, high-fiving and hugging their teammates. Senior leaders embracing the learning experience with childlike enthusiasm.

Two days they had spent analysing reports, crafting strategies and making operating decisions for their simulated business. It was just a story, but at the same time, so much more than that. They got to play the leading role in the story, and together they determined the way forward. The strategy was uniquely theirs, and so was the journey that followed.

They had relied on each other for insight and information. Some team members had monitored the financial statements, while others had focused on opportunities and trends. They had experimented together and taken risks. They had evaluated results together, both the good and the bad. They had laughed together. They had cried together. There was a magic in the room as the minds of individuals connected with their teammates as they rose to the challenge, together. They learnt from each other, and they learnt from the experience. It was not the simulation, but them connecting as humans that turned the learning into an experience they will never forget.

It is because of experiences like these that I am passionate about business simulations.

This is what learning about business and strategy should look and feel like.

Unfortunately, most of the time, it doesn't. Oftentimes, we rely on traditional learning methods, which can be dull, boring or unrelatable. To help engagement, we might bring in external facilitators, who are great at facilitating but don't have a deep understanding of our business or a close connection to our strategy. And even if we find knowledgeable speakers that can inspire an audience, it can be difficult for individuals to know what to do next. People leave the session inspired, but as soon as they return to the drudgeries of their day to day, that inspiration fades quickly.

Traditional approaches, such as expert speakers or the written word, will always play an important role in strategy education. But relying on these teaching methods alone may not be sufficient to help people develop the capabilities they need to be able to make good strategic choices.

Typically, we don't associate gameplay with learning. Why not? Traditionally, we think of gameplay as something we do just for fun, while learning needs to be hard. We need to focus, pay attention, take in and retain information.

According to Peter Senge, author of *The Fifth Discipline*, the word 'learning' has become synonymous with taking in information. Taking in information is, however, only distantly related to real learning. Real learning requires us to be engaged and experience the impact of our decisions and actions.

As humans, we cannot learn by being passive spectators; we need to engage, experiment and use our own reason to make sense of the world.

Learning is not simply transmitting content. It doesn't have to be heavy textbooks, boring lectures or a sage on a stage. Learners need to be encouraged to find their own way and make their own meaning.

If you are responsible for developing people capability in your teams, your division or your organisation, no doubt you will want to ensure that your people have the ability to make great choices.

Success for any organisations is reliant on good decision making by its people.

Business simulations allow us to translate real-world business challenges into a gripping experience, where learners can engage with strategy and seek answers for themselves. Rather than telling people what to do, we get to create interactive experiences that allow people to draw their own conclusions; the facilitator is merely the guide along the journey.

WHAT IS A BUSINESS SIMULATION?

A simulation is a simplification of reality intended to promote understanding. It is a learning tool that helps us practise our response to a business challenge, in a condensed amount of time and without risk.

Just like pilots use flight simulators for training purposes, so can business leaders practise their skillset in a simulated business world.

Business simulations come in a variety of formats and levels of sophistication. You can think of the simulation tool like a sophisticated version of a monopoly boardgame, but with a different storyline. Typically, simulation tools are computer based, but boardgame versions or hybrids are also possible.

However, there is more to a simulation experience than just the simulation tool. The tool is critical, but the experience is a combination of several methodologies – case studies, group discussions, decision making, debrief sessions, insight sessions and expert speakers. All these activities make up the learning experience.

Every simulation experience looks different, and I have seen many variations since I was first introduced to simulations. In many cases, however, the learning event will follow a similar process. Let me share with you what that looks like from a participant perspective.

It has been several years since I had the opportunity to be a participant, but I still remember the workshop as if it were yesterday. Here is a summary of what the experience looked and felt like for me.

I attended a two-day workshop with approximately twenty other participants. We were grouped into five teams and told that our teams would be competing against each other. We introduced ourselves to our new teammates. We bonded quickly, immediately eager to outperform our peers.

Introduction – Our teams received a case study that was centred around a fictitious telecommunications business. The case study outlined the challenge, gave us context and provided some background information. The facilitator explained the rules and introduced us to the simulation tool, and off we went...

Strategy discussion – We huddled together in our team to devise a strategy. How were we going to win this thing? How would we outperform our peers? We carefully checked all the available information for any clues that might give us a competitive edge. We did our analysis, evaluated our options and set targets. Soon, our little war room was covered in flipchart paper and Post-it notes, on which we had plotted our path to success.

Decision making – After some intense discussion and strategising, we fired up the simulation software. As we punched a few decisions into our simulation tool, we could see the numbers on the profit and loss statement update. The ratios on our dashboard changed. The financial statements were shown both in graphs and as numbers. It was visual, interactive and it was so easy to follow what was happening.

The exercise was about developing a strategy and making business decisions, but at the same time the simulation tool made financial concepts easy to understand. We borrowed money, invested money and made operating decisions. We created and sold products, hired staff and invested in marketing. The financial statements and ratios were simply an output – the result of the decisions we had made.

Results debrief – We ran our fictitious business over three rounds (or three simulated years in the realm of our virtual world). After each round, the facilitator shared the results. It was all about us. We cared about the results; we wanted to know how they compared against other teams. We wanted to know what they meant. Understanding financial statements and ratios was important. We wanted to win. The facilitator had our undivided attention.

Insight sessions – Our strategy did not always play out as we had hoped. How could we improve our results? We were thirsty for knowledge! The facilitator shared insights about strategy, finance and value creation. Theory sessions had immediate applicability; we could apply the insights in our next decision round.

Expert advice – Over the course of our two-day workshop, we had two guest speakers. The first was Mark, the company CEO; the other was Alex, an HR executive. Both speakers gave us an insight into their day-to-day roles and shared their views on strategy. They spoke about business challenges from their perspective and shared their unique insight. Because we had just worked through our own strategic challenges in our simulated world, it was easy to relate to their stories.

As mentioned earlier, every simulation experience looks different. But if you have never had a chance to experience a simulation workshop yourself, then I hope my story gives you a little more insight into what the experience looks and feels like. Throughout the rest of the book, we will delve deeper into why these experiences can help us build the necessary skills to allow us to realise the benefits of our strategy.

HOW THIS BOOK WILL BENEFIT YOU

If it is your responsibility to invest in people capability for your teams, your division or your organisation, then this is arguably one of the most critical decisions you can make for the business. After all, in a knowledge-based economy, people talent is key!

Collectively, people need to be making great decisions that are aligned with your business's strategy.

The aim of a business simulation experience is to help you fulfill that objective. But to achieve the full potential of what a simulation experience may be able to deliver, method and message need to work together in harmony. Only if learners are able to make meaning for themselves will the experience result in behaviour change.

This book addresses these topics – method, message and meaning. Its aim is to give you a deeper insight into the value of business simulations and some of the pitfalls to watch out for. Investing in a simulation experience is a big and important decision. This book will provide you with insights and spark some ideas that will allow you to evaluate whether a business simulation experience might be the right approach for you and your teams.

Your strategy is important. You spare no effort in crafting a good strategy! The next step is to ensure that your people do not just understand your strategy, but also have an opportunity to engage with it.

It is not enough to tell people the benefits of the strategy; they need to experience it and make it their own.

If you want your people to be more empowered and be better prepared to tackle the business challenges of tomorrow, business simulations are powerful tools that allow you to set up your people for success.

This book is just the beginning of a conversation. It is a suggested approach for strategy education, with a few examples that help paint a clearer picture and that might spark some ideas. Ultimately, the conversation needs to be centred around you and your strategy. And that requires further discussion.

For now, this book seeks to address a few questions you might have about business simulations:

- What is the benefit of the learning methodology?
- How do they help us overcome real-world learning challenges?
- What kind of business challenges can a simulation experience address?
- What might be the appropriate solution for your target audience?
- How does the experience drive behavioural change?

WHY I WROTE THIS BOOK

The purpose of this book is to explain how the miracle of engaging learning experiences can change the way we see and engage with the world. Business simulations are powerful tools that allow us to immerse ourselves in a learning experience unlike any other. Yet, the simulation itself is just a form of authoring. Just like books, you will find stories that resonate with you and stories that don't. Some are beautifully written, while others can be hard to follow. When we choose books, we look for stories with a compelling narrative, one that speaks to us and our problems. In the same way, a business simulation needs to connect with our reality. Relevance is key!

The purpose of this book is not to talk about how to build simulations. Rather, the purpose is to focus on why simulations allow us to learn more deeply compared to most other learning methodologies. We will explore how a simulation experience can help us develop the skillsets that we will need to be able to tackle the business challenges of the future.

I believe that simulations, in general, will play an increasingly important role in all aspects of education as our world becomes more interconnected and trickier to understand. The examples I share are only a small subset of what is possible. There is much more that exists and much more yet to explore. The purpose is simply to start the conversation and to share insights and ideas around how we might create the stories that help us prepare for the challenges ahead.

Are you ready?
Let's explore!

THE CHALLENGE
WITH LEARNING

THE OTHER DAY, I CAME ACROSS AN IDEA THAT RESONATED deeply with me. It was in one of the concluding chapters of Chris Anderson's book *TED Talks*. The chapter is about the 'talk renaissance' that we are experiencing, and about how learning from different domains of knowledge helps us develop our understanding of the world and allows us to connect ideas in new ways.

In the chapter, Anderson makes an interesting observation. It is about how, as a result of advances in technology, machine learning and AI, the type of knowledge that we humans require is very different from what the Industrial Age asked of us. He talks about how specialist knowledge will increasingly be replaced, supported or improved by computers. But, interestingly, he claims that as the demand on us humans to perform repetitive tasks decreases and specialist knowledge becomes more easily accessible, the need for understanding is ever increasing.

This immediately piqued my interest. I've always been curious about what skillsets the future will demand from us and how we will need to reinvent ourselves and our organisations for the challenges that lie ahead. Anderson speaks about three domains of knowledge that are likely to increase in importance.

Firstly, he suggests that it is likely that there will be an increased demand for more systems-level strategic thinking, requiring the understanding of how individual ideas connect together in the bigger picture. Second, there will be an increased demand for human creativity. It reminded me of Sir Ken Robinson's TED Talk on creativity in education, in which he claims that '...*creativity now is as important in education as literacy.*' The third observation is that we need to develop a much deeper understanding of our own humanity.

It got me thinking about how we develop the people skills that we will need to ensure our businesses are prepared for a vastly different future.

> *When hands are replaced by machines, business becomes less about the quality and efficiency of production and more about how we manage the complexity of relationships in an ever-changing network.*

So how do we build the skillset that we'll need for the challenges of the future?

People will need to learn how to lead in environments of complexity. We need to understand how a decision in one area of the business impacts the rest of the business and the wider network in which we operate. But there are several reasons why learning to lead in complexity is impossible or impractical in the real world. We need to overcome some of these real-world learning challenges.

PROBLEM 1: LIMITED LEARNING OPPORTUNITIES

We learn from mistakes. But in the real world, the consequences of mistakes can be fatal. We don't want to put lives, jobs or our company at risk for the sake of learning.

However, even if the consequences are negligible, we typically do not encourage or incentivise risk taking. If you work in a large enterprise, risk avoidance is typically the safer route. We choose the safe route to avoid feeling vulnerable and exposed. Testing a new idea in the real world has consequences. And traditional organisations are typically unforgiving when it comes to making mistakes.

Another learning challenge for large, complex organisations is that we're often far removed from seeing the consequences of our choices.

The most powerful learning comes from direct experience. We do something that puts a smile on a customer's face, and we know we've done well. Or we see the disappointment in the eyes of another, and we know we've messed up. But what happens when we can no longer see the consequences of our actions?

And even if we do get feedback, the value of that feedback is often lost due to time delays. In the real world, the consequences of our decisions can sometimes stretch on for years or even decades. Have you ever worked in an organisation where the wrong person has been promoted into a leadership position? Even if we come to the realisation that we made the wrong choice, it can take years to resolve. It's a costly mistake if we have to wait, say, ten years until that person retires and then have another go. Imagine if we could learn the same lesson in a matter of hours, rather than a couple of years or decades.

PROBLEM 2: FLAWED ASSUMPTIONS

In our everyday jobs, we are required to make decisions. We are required to react to events as they unfold. We don't always have the perfect insight into any given situation, so we make assumptions. They are calculated guesses that help us plug the knowledge gap and find a good-enough solution that will make do, for now. We might also simply follow a predefined process with little thought – we just act. Someone developed that process for a reason, right?

Furthermore, it is easy to be tempted by decisions that have immediate benefit to ourselves. Like being persuaded to say yes to an opportunity that helps us make our quarterly numbers. However, we find ourselves in a dangerous place when these decisions are made without a deep understanding of the system-wide consequences and the impact on other aspects such as relationships, trust and culture.

Consciously or unconsciously, we draw on existing mental models to help us make decisions. But since we don't have anything to compare our decision against, we are often unaware of the flaws in our assumptions.

We need a space for learning in which we can contrast and compare the impact of different choices.

We need a safe space in which people don't need to be defensive about their chosen course of action, but where it is safe to explore new ideas and different possibilities.

PROBLEM 3: BOUNDED RATIONALITY

In business, being big can provide significant advantages, such as bargaining power, economies of scale and brand loyalty, for example. But the bigger we get, the more complex our world becomes. When we're engulfed in this complexity, we can easily lose sight of what truly matters. Our day-to-day reality becomes a whirlwind of activity, with meetings, crises and phone calls demanding our immediate attention. We're reacting to a bombardment of challenges. We're not learning when we're distracted by noise.

To figure out what kind of approaches might work for us, we need a good understanding of how our organisations behave and how we would like them to behave. We need to be able to evaluate our decisions in the context of the big picture. However, we are constrained by what systems theorists refer to as bounded rationality – our ability to reason is limited by the limitations of the human mind itself. When we are faced with an overwhelming amount of complexity in the real world, our limited cognitive capabilities force us to fall back on routine procedures, habits, rules of thumb and simple mental models.

What if we could remove some of the complexity to help us better understand the consequences of our decisions?

What if we could deal with scenarios in a space where we can test our assumptions, take risks and learn from mistakes? Instead of guessing, what if we had a space in which we could start testing?

THE POWER OF BUSINESS SIMULATIONS

Simulations are the perfect tool to help us create clarity in complexity. They allow us to make sense of the bigger picture and explore ideas in a safe space. Business simulations are not designed to help us predict the future or to tell us what to do. They are a learning methodology that allows us to experiment, test and discover. Into this learning methodology, we need to embed a powerful message – a story that speaks to our audience and allows them to make meaning based on the context in which they lead.

Figure 1: A business simulation experience

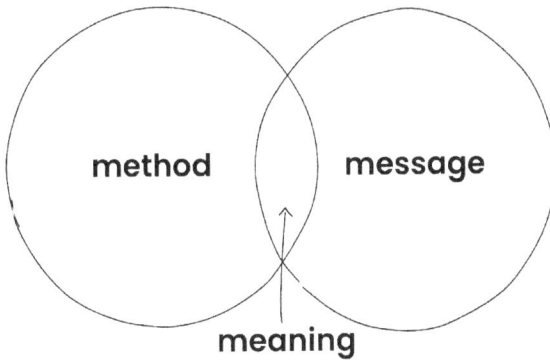

There is a lot more to a business simulation experience than just a fancy piece of software that allows us to play a business game.

Done right, a business simulation can transform an audience's worldview.

Throughout this book we will unpack how the combination of method and message allows us to create these impactful experiences. Experiences that allow people to make strategy their own.

Let me briefly define the labels of the model in *Figure 1: A business simulation experience.*

Method – is all about the simulation. Not just the game component, but rather the overall experience. As discussed in the introduction, there are several elements to this – gameplay, discussion sessions, results debriefs, insight sessions and speaker sessions. In this book we will explore how business simulations are different to traditional learning. We will explore how they allow us to capture attention, shift perspective and develop our adaptability skills through risk-free practice.

Message – is all about the story. The best way to think of designing a simulation experience is to look at it as a form of authoring. That means that the possibilities for the types of *message* we can craft are endless.

In Part 2, I will share three examples of the kind of *messages* we can imbed in our simulation solutions. The following chapter, *The challenge for business*, will set the scene for the problems that have inspired these sample solutions.

Meaning – happens when we strike the right balance between method and message. It's about creating a learning event that resonates with people's real-world challenges. Being able to make the connection between what is being shared in the simulation experience and people's day to day allows learners to make meaning.

TAPPING INTO OUR POTENTIAL

The type of knowledge that we will need to navigate the business challenges that lie ahead will look vastly different to the type of knowledge we've needed in the past. Our need for specialist knowledge will increasingly be aided by computers and artificial intelligence.

However, our need for understanding is ever increasing, meaning we need to develop a better understanding of our systems, our creativity potential and our own humanity.

How do we best go about developing those capabilities? It's a question we will seek to address throughout the rest of the book. Before we go there, however, let us explore some of the challenges for business and the understanding we need to develop to navigate our complex world.

that is bigger than conforming to what is expected of them. By immersing themselves in poetry, they discovery a deeper sense of their own humanity; they tap into their creative capacities and discover a deeper sense of meaning beyond the clear path that has been set out for them.

They start believing in themselves and that their ideas matter. But as they do, they are confronted by people in positions of authority who do not share that point of view and do not buy into their dreams and visions. Whether it is the parents, other teachers or the school principle – they are more interested in maintaining the status quo. They will not risk losing the safe career path to teenage dreamers. Parents have made sacrifices for their children's education and they want to control the outcomes. Their characters defend a system that is a stark reminder of Taylorism. A belief system in which the world is divided into professions that separate the thinkers at the top from the doers at the bottom. Parents who have seen the harsh reality of a life in toil and struggle will not risk an uncertain path. Nothing and no one will tell them otherwise. They want to guarantee that their sons secure a place at the top.

It is an important story because it reminds us that a change in perspective can transform the way we see the world and how we engage with it.

But the story also carries a message of caution. Just because we have expanded our horizons and have seen things from a bigger perspective, it does not mean others are ready or willing to share our views. When we lead with courage, it requires an awareness of the things that are important to those around us. Even a change for the better might seem like a threat to those that seek stability

THE CHALLENGE
FOR BUSINESS

HAVE YOU HAVE EVER WORKED IN AN ORGANISATION, OR IN a division, where senior leaders have proposed a new strategy or idea, and you've instinctively had that gut feeling it wasn't going to fly?

A couple of months ago, I was interviewing Rob, a client relationship manager working for a large financial institution. His division had appointed a new leader, and I was interested to hear how the implementation of the new strategy was going. Part of the change was structural, and it meant changing the way clients were allocated to account managers. When I asked Rob how things were going, he said that he'd spoken to his colleague and they had decided among themselves that they were not going to bother and instead keep allocations the way they were. He said that another leadership change and a new strategy would probably happen within the next two years and disrupting the client relationships that had been built over the years just didn't make sense.

Sound familiar? It doesn't mean that the strategy wasn't sound; it just didn't fit with the way people were thinking, acting and engaging with others. When you've been building relationships based on trust for years, it's unlikely you're going to be keen to shift behaviour, just because someone who's been appointed into a new leadership role suddenly has a new idea.

Relationship manager Rob didn't want to be difficult or to stand in the way of progress. He was just not convinced that the idea was that great. And he might have been right. Trust does take years to build. And it has immense value! But trust isn't something that shows up on the spreadsheet that might have been used to devise a better way of allocating accounts.

As individuals, teams and organisations, we do need to evolve; we do need to change – and that requires both Rob and his boss to see things from each other's perspective and to be open to new ideas.

Command-and-control won't work; maintaining the status quo won't work – both individuals need to understand, align and rise up, together.

WE NEED TO EVOLVE

Looking back at how organisations have evolved throughout history allows us to make sense of both the present and the challenges that lie ahead. I loved reading the opening chapters of *Reinventing Organisations* by Frederic Laloux. He gives the reader a tour of past organisational models and describes the shifting paradigms that have shaped our evolutionary journey – from small family bands with belief systems shaped by magic and spirits to religion and powerful chiefdoms, science and scalable organisational structures.

As our worldviews and organisational systems evolve, each era brings with it a light side and a dark side. Progress is always marred by uncertainty.

This useful reflection helps us understand that evolving and adapting to changes in the operating environment isn't new. We've been doing it for thousands of years. We are confronted with choices as we head into an uncertain future. Sometimes, organisations pick the wrong path and need to course-correct, often at great expense. Famous case studies from our recent history, such as Nokia, Kodak and Blockbuster, remind us of this.

When belief systems change, when worldviews change, when customer preferences change, are we able to let go of what we have learnt and the things we believe to be true? It can be extremely difficult to disidentify from something we were previously engulfed in. Are we able to return to a beginner's mindset? Are we willing to unlearn?

'I must reduce myself to zero.'

– MAHATMA GANDHI

There are two words that Laloux uses in the opening chapters of his book that I find particularly useful in the context of describing shifting worldviews – the words are 'evolution' and 'maturity'. I like them because it isn't about right or wrong. It's not about having the 'right' belief system; it's about being able to step into a worldview that is appropriate for our time. More maturity is not better than less maturity, but it is our ability to evaluate risks and make decisions that have consequences for others.

The reason we don't give everyone full autonomy to do whatever they like in an organisation is similar to the reason we don't allow minors to drive motor vehicles. It is not about technical capability; it's about our ability to anticipate risks, understand consequences and take accountability.

The ability of our organisations to evolve and keep pace with change increases when we distribute authority to individuals on the frontline, where the action and the information is. But just like we need guidance and a safe space when learning to drive, we need a space in which leaders can practise decision making and hone their business skills. A space where it is safe to learn.

What we need is to be able to trust people to make decisions in the moment as unexpected events unfold.

Let us take a moment to assess our current situation. What are some of the problems that are holding us back? We all want to be agile and adaptive, but what kind of barriers do we need to overcome, and why does it matter?

PROBLEM 1: OUR ORGANISATIONS ARE NOT IN GOOD SHAPE

Uncertainty and the pace of change are themes that will be addressed in several sections of this book. But the problem for organisations is not uncertainty or the pace of change – these are not things that we can fix. The problem is that our organisations are not in good shape to cope with the challenges that the environment is posing.

If we were to do an organisational health check on our own

organisation, it is likely that we'd find some concerning symptoms. Here are just a few examples from recent business literature and new articles. (These are just for the sake of illustration; no doubt, we'd be able to add to this list.)

- The life expectancy for large organisations is declining, significantly. According to research by Richard Foster and Innosight, the average lifespan of leading US companies has decreased by more than fifty years in the last century – from sixty-seven years in the 1920s to just fifteen years today.
- We get caught off guard – incidents such as floods, bushfires and COVID-19 force us to hatch a Plan B on the fly. We struggle to predict what is going to happen even in relatively short time horizons. Rigid plans are pointless; our ability to adapt is critical.
- People do not trust their leaders. A survey, published by Forbes, found that sixty-five per cent of employees would forgo a pay raise if it meant seeing their leader fired. If this is the level of distrust, what does that say about our ability to endure challenging times?
- Well-intentioned incentives can backfire. The *Harvard Business Review* article 'Don't Let Metrics Undermine Your Business' suggests that our reward mechanisms can lead to unethical behaviour. In one of the studies, employees under investigation cited the relentless pressure to achieve challenging sales targets as the main reason for misconduct.

We want our organisations to be more agile and adaptive, but the company culture and systems that we typically find in legacy organisations suggest that we are not in good shape to weather the storms ahead.

PROBLEM 2: PARADIGMS OF THE PAST ARE HOLDING US BACK

When we step into a leadership role, we inherit systems that were designed by those that came before us. But what kind of thinking shaped these systems? Many have their roots in an age in which the challenges of the world looked vastly different. What if they no longer serve us?

As I was scanning some of the recent literature on organisational change, I came across a story that kept reappearing in multiple sources. It's the story of Frederick Winslow Taylor and his *Principles of Scientific Management*. Here is a brief summary to help illustrate the point around belief systems and how they have shaped the world as we know it.

In the early 1900s, Frederick Winslow Taylor introduced *The Scientific Approach to Management* to the world. *Taylorism*, as it is often referred to, brought on some of the most influential beliefs in the history of management. It is the belief that we can manage organisations like complicated systems, systems of cause and effect, much like a machine. By timing every procedure on the shop floor, tweaking actions and timing again, this 'scientific' approach allowed the massive machines of industry to produce high-quality goods at low cost. An approach of rigorous, reductionist optimisation and standardisation. Every little procedure could be studied and predicted and, therefore, controlled. It allowed for the systematic elimination of variation. But it also signified the end of autonomy for workers. They were not expected to understand why or how things worked. The managers had already done the thinking for them; all that was required from the workers was to execute.

The scientific approach to management was widely adopted because it brought a beautiful simplicity to a chaotic world. It gave us the ability to control disorder and to predict outcomes. It allowed us to create plans and budgets and bring a level of certainty to our unpredictable world.

It's undeniable that the levels of prosperity we enjoy today would not be possible without advances such as these. In the last century, we have shifted from a world of scarcity to a world of abundance. And so, we find ourselves in a world where we cling to these paradigms of the past. Many of these principles are still present all around us, every day. Whether it's the robot-like greeting you get at the drive-through or the way you are treated in your hospital bed following surgery – how you are treated and how long it should take has already been carefully calculated and predetermined by someone else.

The problem is that principles such as 'the scientific approach' might be useful for efficiency and consistency, but these principles don't allow us to respond to changing needs, and they leave no room for adaptivity. Responsiveness and adaptability, however, are precisely the qualities we look for in our fast-paced, uncertain world. The person best placed to determine how you, the customer, should be served or treated is the person on the frontline, not some manager back at head office.

Today, we are less concerned about scarcity and more concerned about overshoots and inequity. And while the problems that we are facing in the world today are changing rapidly, the systems we have inherited are informed by paradigms of the past. How do we rise to the challenge of the problems of the future? And what are the paradigms holding us back?

Our problems have changed, but our systems have not.

Our ability to act fast is critical. But our control mechanisms are not only stifling, but also send a clear message that employees can't be trusted. Even simple actions require management approval. Our policy overreach is weighing us down. We are great at creating policies, but not so good at decluttering.

> *'We are being asked to invent the future, but to do so inside a culture of work that is deeply broken.'*
>
> – AARON DIGNAN

PROBLEM 3: WE ARE NOT REALISING THE BENEFITS OF OUR STRATEGY

It is not by accident that the quote 'culture eats strategy for breakfast', typically attributed to late management consultant Peter Drucker, has found much resonance in business writing. Organisations have always struggled with bridging the gap between strategy formulation and effective day-to-day implementation. Given the rapid pace of change, for many organisations, this gap is widening significantly.

Larry Bossidy and Ram Charan, authors of *Execution – The Discipline of Getting Things Done,* claim that *execution* is the biggest issue facing business today. When companies fail to deliver on their promises, we often reason that the strategy was wrong. However, the strategy itself is often not the cause. Bossidy and Charan argue that, most often, strategies fail because they are not executed well.

This claim is supported by research in other business publications, including the *Harvard Business Review* and the *Economist Intelligence Unit*, which suggest that around two-thirds of strategic initiatives fail to deliver the desired performance results. In other words, no matter how smart your strategy, without buy-in from your teams, it's unlikely you'll realise its benefits.

We need to overcome these execution challenges. We need to build the capability that ensures we can turn ideas into action and remove the stifling bureaucratic systems that are holding us back.

We need to ensure people are acting in ways that are aligned with strategy, rather than acting in their self-interest and pulling in different directions.

ALIGNMENT & EVOLUTION

A fast-paced world demands from us an ability to react in the moment. We don't have the luxury of time; we don't get the benefit of hindsight. We need to build the confidence to be able to play in such environments, knowing when we can use our judgement and when we need help. We need to be able to navigate our complex world with dexterity. For decades, we've been avoiding complexity, by managing our organisations like machines – systems of cause and effect. We need to train ourselves to be comfortable with complexity. Simulations are the perfect tool. They make the complex less daunting and help us build the confidence we need to make good decisions and steer the right course.

The *alignment & evolution* model (Figure 2) shows the need for our organisations to be able to evolve to meet the needs of an ever-changing environment. We need to develop the appropriate level of maturity across strategy, people and systems to be able to keep up with the pace of change.

Figure 2: The alignment & evolution model

The Environment	Strategy	People	Systems
disruptive	adaptive	autonomous	networked
uncertain	responsive	empowered	connected
predictable	competitive	task-driven	efficient
stable	scalable	compliant	controlling

The labels inside the model are simply signposts for the type of behaviour or culture you might expect at the different levels. I often encourage clients or participants to make the language their own. More important than the labels are the dimensions – the vertical and the horizontal. The vertical shift is about evolution; the horizontal is about alignment.

As we move upwards on the model, we shift from an environment that is predictable and doesn't change very fast to one that is fast-changing and likely to surprise us. To be able to cope with increasing levels of uncertainty in our environment, our strategy needs to evolve, and so do our people and systems.

The other critical part is that we are aligned. Only if we're aligned across strategy, people and systems can we cope with the demands of the environment. No matter how good the strategy, it is not going to succeed unless we can bring people along on the journey, and we're not going to thrive unless we have enabling systems in place that will support us.

Just like Laloux's history lesson on evolving worldviews, none of these levels is 'right' or 'wrong'. The question is whether we have the necessary maturity to operate at a level that is appropriate for our environment.

Let us explore the levels in a little more detail.

LEVEL 1: STABLE

If we operate in an environment that doesn't change very fast, we might choose a strategy that allows our products and services to be delivered at scale. We want to ensure they can be sold to as many customers as possible and that the quality is consistent. We need people that comply with the quality standards that we have set, and we need systems that ensure the strategy is executed as planned. At this level, we don't have many competitors and, therefore, the need for differentiation is low. Picture the world of Henry Ford in 1909. Ford is reported to have said, 'You can have your car painted any colour you want, as long as it's black.'

LEVEL 2: PREDICTABLE

When more players enter the market and we are vying for the attention of the same customers, our ability to differentiate is key. We need a competitive strategy, something that sets us apart from the rest. We achieve that differentiation either by offering more value or a better price. But as our industry matures, value differentiation becomes increasingly difficult.

Think of the banking industry, for example. Do the big banks have something that clearly sets them apart from the rest? In the absence of value differentiation, we compete primarily on price. To survive in this undifferentiated marketplace, we need to be more efficient. We reward people for driving commercial outcomes; the focus is often on delivering short-term financial results. Our systems are structured for efficiency and low cost.

LEVEL 3: UNCERTAIN

As the rate of change increases, we need to implement strategies that are responsive. The focus is not only on commercial outcomes, but also a recognition that we need to balance the needs of a multitude of stakeholders. Strategies are typically more long-term focused, with an appreciation for the value of relationships. We are more focused on creating customer loyalty, employee engagement and community trust. We use tools such as the balanced scorecard to measure performance. We think beyond our corporate boundaries and have systems that connect smartly with customers and suppliers. We invest in data-mining technologies to help us understand the landscape and recognise patterns.

LEVEL 4: DISRUPTIVE

The final level is about adaptability. It is about our ability to create effective strategies at the network level. We view the organisation in the context of the entire ecosystem in which it operates and find ways that allow strategies to evolve without necessarily being able to rely on strong control mechanisms. We create guiding principles that foster interaction with minimal barriers. It's about generating trust among participants, providing transparency and pushing responsibility to the edges of the organisation, where the action and information is.

PLAYING A SUCCESSFUL GAME

A common challenge for businesses is that we are all operating in an environment that is vastly different from anything we've known before. Adapting to this fast-paced and uncertain world is tricky, since many of the systems and processes that we have inherited were created during a time when our environment was different and world was a lot less connected.

We will need strategies that allow us to play a successful game in an uncertain and disruptive world. But an adaptive strategy alone will not be enough. Our actions across the organisation need to be aligned. We need learning experiences that help us understand what that looks like, so we can bring our best game!

We need to ensure the decisions we make are aligned and help move our organisation in the right direction.

Let's explore how we might be able to leverage the power of business simulation to help us get prepared.

WHAT'S NEXT?

THE REST OF THE BOOK FOLLOWS THE MESSAGE, METHOD and meaning structure that we introduced in Chapter 1. Each of these sections has its own model. Below, *Figure 3: The key framework* offers a high-level overview of how these sections relate to each other.

Figure 3: The key framework

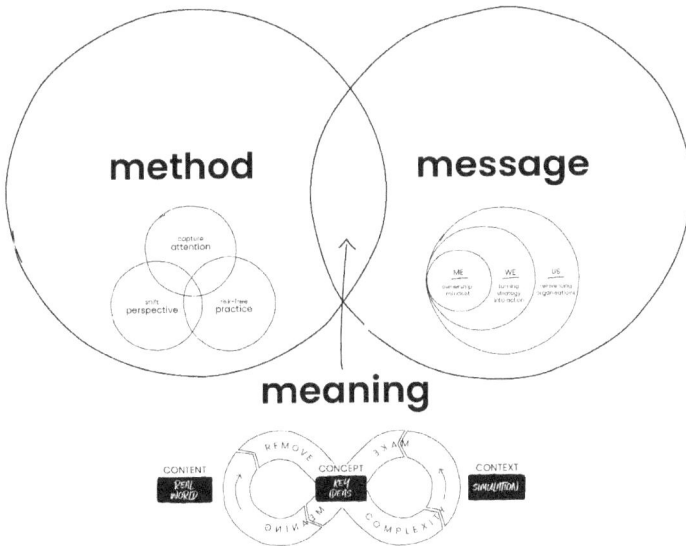

Here is a brief synopsis of what will be covered in each of these parts:

Part 1: Method – talks about business simulations as a learning methodology. This section seeks to answer why method plays a crucial role in helping us develop the skillsets we need for our complex and fast-changing world. We will explore how business simulations allow us to capture attention and what that means for learning. We will discover how a shift perspective can change the way we see and engage with the world. And we will explore how practising in a risk-free environment can help us develop our adaptability skills.

Part 2: Message – is about the story or narrative we design into the simulation experience. The message can be crafted in an infinite number of ways and it will typically relate to your unique strategy. But to give you a sense of what this might look like, I share three examples that speak to the *challenge for business* that we just discussed in Chapter 2. How do we play a successful *above-the-line* game on the *alignment & evolution* model? We will look at this challenge from three different perspectives. What does it mean for frontline leaders, mid-level managers and senior/exec leaders?

Part 3: Meaning – is about translating concepts from our virtual world back into the real world. If method and message work together in harmony, simulations allow us to make meaning. And if we can make meaning, we can take action. This is the critical last step that facilitates behavioural change.

PART 1

METHOD

WHEN IT COMES TO LEARNING, IT'S NOT JUST ABOUT THE quality of information available to us, but also how we engage with it. Simulations allow us to turn information into something that is visual and interactive. We get to add a competitive dynamic. And, most importantly, we allow learners to go on a journey and craft a story that is their own.

While other people's stories can inspire us, it is our own individual experiences that ultimately drive behaviour change. We need experiences that allow us not only to take in new information, but also to make it relevant for our own situation. In the simulated world, we get to experiment with new ideas and learn through a process of experimentation and iteration. Rather than being told what the right way is, we get to discover solutions for ourselves. It's a process through which we get to make meaning that is relevant to us as individuals.

Figure 4: Experiences that shift behaviour

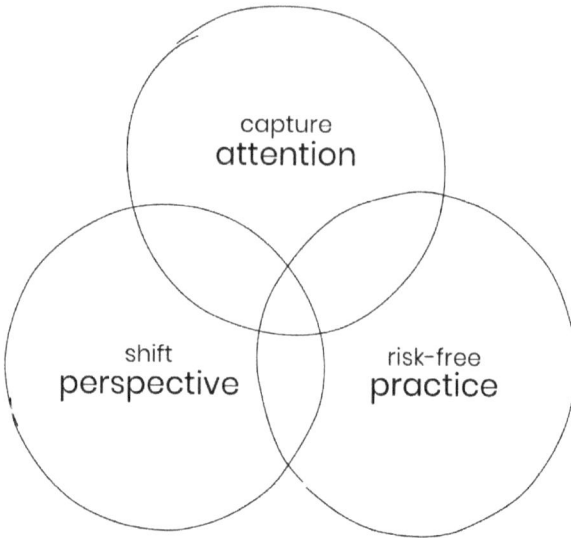

Simulations allow us to create learning experiences unlike any other. In the following chapters, we talk about some of the specific benefits that the methodology brings to leadership development, with specific focus on the following key themes:

- Simulations allow us to turn information into interactive experiences that grab our **attention**. We want to create stories in which we get to play the leading role. It is all about us as learners – our decisions, our discovery, our journey.
- We get to immerse ourselves in an experience in which we are removed from the busyness of our day to day. The simulation allows us to **shift perspective** and see problems in a new light. When we strip away the complexities of the real world, we get to focus on just a few core ideas, ideas that really matter.
- Learning in a **risk-free** environment allows us to hone our adaptability potential, our ability to respond to the inevitability

of change. We get to consider several versions of a possible future and, thereby, **practise** and prepare for some of the business challenges that lie ahead.

We will explore how simulations help us make sense of our turbulent world. We will discover how they allow us to better understand the big picture and evaluate the impact of our decisions.

CAPTURE ATTENTION

WE LIVE IN A WORLD WHERE WE ARE FLOODED WITH INFOR-mation. We have an extraordinary amount of exceptional knowledge at our fingertips, whenever we want it. With all the content that is being created, books published, articles written, videos posted, the most amazing talks from all over the world — much of it instantly accessible at no cost — surely, we have all the knowledge we'll ever need. In fact, it is so much that it can feel overwhelming. How do we separate the junk from the good stuff? What deserves our attention and what doesn't?

When we think about how best to develop our leaders for the future, we spend a lot of time obsessing about message, and perhaps not enough time obsessing about method. Leadership development is not just about sharing information, but also about the process through which we engage with it.

I came across a quote the other day in which author Tiago Forte suggests that 'people's attention is a more scarce resource than money.'

In the context of learning, that is a useful insight. If I think back to my school days, teachers often reprimanded me for not paying attention. But when I think about some of the best teachers I had, it was different – they would capture my attention; it did not feel like I needed to make an effort to 'pay' attention. I think that, as educators, attention is partly our responsibility. It is not enough to have a clever message or idea; it needs to be delivered in a way that resonates with our audience. We need to give learners a reason to care.

We should think of attention not as something that is paid, but rather as something that is captured.

We need teaching methods to help us engage with information more deeply. We can think about learning experiences across two dimensions. The first has to do with participation (either active or passive), and the second with connection (either absorption or immersion). For example, we can absorb knowledge by reading a book (active) or watching a video (passive), or we can get immersed in an experience like attending a lecture (passive) or playing a game (active).

Stories can inspire us. Lectures can help us close a knowledge gap. But engaging stories and lectures are rare. You have to be a skilled author, speaker or actor to be able to hold our attention for an extended period of time. We have all attended those lectures where the only thing that caught our attention was our head tipping over, as we slowly dozed off...

Active immersion is different. We know from personal experience that it is much easier to capture and hold our attention when the story is about us, and when we get to play a part in the narrative!

*'Knowledge cannot be pushed into a brain; it
needs to be pulled in.'*

– CHRIS ANDERSON, HEAD OF TED

A TURBULENT WORLD

Today we live in a world where the rate of change exceeds the rate at which we can learn or take in new information. In his TED Talk 'Smart failure for a fast-changing world', Eddie Obeng shares a metaphor that helps paint a picture of what has happened to our ability to learn in a turbulent environment. He asks us to imagine a transparent pipe, through which water is flowing. Into this pipe we inject a needle and, using a syringe, we push green ink into the flow of water. With consistent water pressure, all we will see is a thin green line as it tracks along with the flow of the water. Nothing too exciting about that. And if we were to increase the water pressure, we might expect our green ink simply to travel at a higher speed, similar to the flow of water. However, that is not what happens. The turbulence created by the increased pressure has changed the rules of the game. Our thin green line doesn't exist anymore. The increased water pressure has created a level of turbulence that has caused eddies around our needle-tip and the green ink disperses in the turbulent waters.

Eddie's point is that a couple of years ago something similar happened in our world; there was a point in time where our environment started changing faster than we as individuals and organisations could learn. The recipe for success in a turbulent world is no longer dependent on our ability to take in more information. Learning in a turbulent world relies on a completely different set of rules.

I believe that traditional teaching methods will always be an important part of learning. It is the way we share information and transmit knowledge.

However, traditional teaching methods alone are not sufficient to prepare us for our turbulent world.

Have you ever been dumped by a big wave while you were swimming or surfing in the ocean? Do you remember that feeling of complete helplessness, where you had no idea which way was up and which way was down? Not sure whether you would be able to hold your breath long enough before finding your way back to the surface? When we're in turbulence, all we care about is survival.

Learning in a simulated world is like learning to swim in turbulent waters. When we zoom out, we recognise patterns in waves. We can see how currents behave so we can work with them, rather than against them.

Just like we don't control the oceans in which we swim, we do not control the networks in which we operate.

We need to understand how systems are likely to behave and how our actions influence their behaviour. We need to make informed decisions, without being able to 'know' the right answers. It is less about knowing and more about understanding.

DESIGNING INTERACTIVE EXPERIENCES

A critical part of creating a compelling narrative is development of the simulation tool – the 'game', so to speak. Regardless of whether the platform is IT based, boardgame based or a hybrid, what is important is that experience strikes the right balance between simplicity and complexity. Too complex and the learning messages are lost; too simple and the audience does not feel challenged. Anyone can build a business simulation, but getting this balance right requires not just technical skills, but experience. It also requires excellent business acumen, as well as a deep understanding of strategy, particularly *your* strategy if it is a customised solution.

There are a lot of moving parts and creating a smooth-running, engaging experience that carries a powerful message is no easy feat. William Hall, author of *Shift: Using Business Simulations and Serious Games*, suggests that you work with a provider you trust, and in whom you have the utmost confidence.

The tool is critical, but a learning experience is not just about the *game* element. A business simulation is not a puzzle to be solved or a race to be won. Or, dare I say, it shouldn't be. It's a story that has twists and turns and unexpected surprises. Every part of the narrative needs to be well thought through and contain a relevant message, crafted specifically for its audience. It allows the learner to explore different paths, but without fear of failure. The facilitator acts only as a guide to ensure that you stay on track and to help your understanding.

Simulations are a story-telling platform in that they allow learners to be actively immersed in the narrative. It is an approach with some tremendously beneficial features, features that allow us to capture and hold people's attention.

VISUAL AND INTERACTIVE

Simulations allow us to make information visual and interactive. They give us dashboards and charts that change as we make decisions. Graphs and reports update live as we experiment with different approaches and possible options.

When information is presented in the right way, things that might sound frighteningly complicated or uninteresting are surprisingly intuitive and easy to grasp. Given the right tools, we can develop a high-level understanding of unfamiliar concepts in a surprisingly short amount of time.

A COMPETITIVE DYNAMIC

We are wired to learn through play. The competitive nature of game-play creates a level of energy and excitement that plays a crucial role in engaging learners. While, arguably, there is no real benefit to 'winning' in the simulation game, it is the rivalry that lifts the energy and turns the entire event into a fun experience. The benefit of gameplay is that it *captures* our attention!

And it also allows for comparison. Without comparison, it is difficult to judge what good looks like. Just like an athlete training for an event, it is through continuous comparison and measurement that we push the boundaries of possibility.

OUR STORY

From my own experience at business school, I know how boring it can be to have to analyse the financial statements of some unknown company.

Business simulations, however, allow us to go on a journey and craft a story that is our own. Perhaps we will set up our organisation for long-term success, or we might focus on pursuing short-term wins. Regardless of whether our decisions are good or bad, we get to see the consequences of our actions; we get to compare and learn from the successes and failures that are uniquely ours.

GAMES THAT CHANGE BEHAVIOUR

In a knowledge-based economy and a fast-changing world, our ability to learn and adapt our behaviour based on changes in context is critical for businesses to be successful. Whether that requires capability building, contextual understanding or a mindset shift, it's about us as learners realising the need and wanting to shift behaviour.

Simulations allow us to create immersive experiences that grab our attention. They draw us in and get us excited about and interested in the message.

If message and method work together in harmony, the need for behaviour change is not forced – it's discovered.

SHIFT PERSPECTIVE

'A mind, once stretched by a new idea, never returns to its original dimensions.'

– RALPH WALDO EMERSON

WHEN I THINK ABOUT THE CONCEPT OF SHIFTING PERSPECTIVE, one of the mental images that comes to mind is that of Robin Williams, in the role of the English teacher Mr. John Keating, standing on top of his classroom desk in the 1989 movie *Dead Poets Society*. 'Why do I stand up here?' he asks his class of students, as they stare up at their newly arrived, liberal-minded teacher. 'I stand up here to remind myself that we must constantly look at things in a different way.'

It is the starting point of a story in which Mr. Keating the English teacher breaks the mould at a strict New England boarding school, to inspire his students to make their lives extraordinary. Keating encourages his students to live life more passionately and with purpose – captured in one of the movie's most famous quotes: '*Carpe diem*. Seize the day.'

As the story unfolds, the students discover their voice, their passions and a vision for the life they aspire to live. It is a journey of discovery in which students get to see the possibilities of a life and prefer the comfort of the status quo. Or, in Mr. Keating's words, 'There is a time for daring, and there is a time for caution. A wise man knows which one is called for.'

A SHIFT IN PERSPECTIVE

Sometimes, a shift in perspective can lead to the most profound personal learning experiences and fundamentally change the way we engage with the world.

When we're busy dealing with our day-to-day challenges – reacting to events and dealing with crises – it can be difficult to be mindful of the bigger picture.

The real world is full of complexity, and it is impossible to know and understand everything and everyone. Problems unfold and escalate quickly; we have to respond to events in the moment. And when the right answer is not immediately available, we have only one choice: We guess.

But the more we can replace assumptions and thoughtless actions with understanding, the better we become at decision making. The challenge is that assumptions are usually unconscious; we don't even know that we are making them. It is the shift in perspective that uncovers them and allows for a more accurate version of reality.

'The real voyage of discovery consists not in seeking new lands but in seeing with new eyes.'

– MARCEL PROUST

When we replace flawed assumptions with new insights, we develop personally and professionally. We get to engage with others from a more considered perspective. This deeper awareness means we can understand others better, be more empathetic and show up in service. We can be more innovative, more creative and more connected.

To help us with this journey of discovery, we need to create experiences that challenge some of the things we believe to be true. We need to be confronted with scenarios that deal with real world problems and understand how our choices impact different stakeholders. We need to experiment, appreciate trade-offs and understand consequences. We need to uncover our biases and find better ways.

UNLEASHING OUR POTENTIAL

As Robin Williams's character says in *Dead Poets Society*, 'No matter what anybody tells you, words and ideas can change the world.' No doubt, technology has transformed our world in the last few decades. Yet, I am taking inspiration from a movie that is more than thirty years old. In 1989, I had not even heard of the internet, nor had I used a mobile phone. It was quite a different world then, yet, the messages from that movie are as relevant today as they were then. It reminds me that it is not technology but ideas that transform our world.

It is important that we believe that our ideas have value, even though, throughout our lives, we will come across those that tell us otherwise. Not only do we need to nurture and hone our creativity skills, we need the courage, confidence and tenacity to turn ideas into reality.

We live in a world that is changing rapidly, yet, our traditional decision hierarchies are typically slow to respond. To be able to operate with agility, we need to ensure that ideas can be acted on by those that are close to the action. Pushing responsibility to the edges of the organisation requires a mindset that is different to the compliance and execution mindset previously asked of frontline leaders. It requires greater levels of accountability and a broader contextual understanding of how the decisions we make impact the organisation as a whole and the multitude of stakeholders we serve.

When authority is distributed to the frontline, and new ideas are tested, mistakes will be made. Mistakes have commercial implications; they have reputational implications. Will we stigmatise mistakes? Are we prepared to be wrong?

In his TED Talk 'Why schools kill creativity', Sir Ken Robinson claims that 'if you're not prepared to be wrong, you'll never come up with anything original'. Unlike adults, he claims kids are not scared to be wrong. But, he argues, by the time we get to be adults, most of us have lost that capacity. In education and in our companies, 'we stigmatize mistakes... we are educating people out of their creative capacities.'

It is difficult to maintain a belief that ideas can change the world when our attempts at making things better receive ferocious criticism. How do we continue to trust our intuition when the feedback we are getting is effectively telling us the opposite of 'your ideas have value'?

To give our ideas a better chance of success, we need to learn how to evaluate them from different angles, and position them accordingly. We need to remove ourselves from the reality we are immersed in and understand how our ideas fit into the broader context of our organisation's priorities.

The realm of simulations allows us to try, to test and to fail. It reminds us that we need to evaluate our ideas not just from our perspective, but from the perspective of all stakeholders that have a vested interest. It reminds us of all the trade-offs we need to consider before we can shape our idea into a goal worth pursuing. We need to create environments in which our ideas have an opportunity to grow.

BETTER CONTEXTUAL UNDERSTANDING

Business simulations go far beyond helping us build more robust commercial acumen. When the storyline connects to real world challenges that we are dealing with in our professions, they allow us to create learning experiences that go deep. A new perspective is an opportunity for better understanding, more clarity, increased curiosity and a more mature worldview.

Putting forward new ideas takes courage. And courage comes from confidence, which we build when we practise, make mistakes, learn and try again. Learning in the real world is hard. And risky. When we remove the obstacles, we can play with possibility, uninhibited by the worries that would otherwise hold us back from exploring, experimenting and trying new things.

Responding to unexpected events in a risk-free space turns the unanticipated difficulties into familiar problems. Through practice, we can build the capabilities that allow for better decision making, faster responses, more accountability, increased levels of ownership and, ultimately, more fulfilment.

RISK-FREE PRACTICE

WE GET CAUGHT OFF GUARD SOMETIMES. AS I AM SITTING here, self-isolating in my apartment as the world responds to COVID-19, I can't help but wonder whether we could have been better prepared. Perhaps it is a risk event that was too hard to anticipate, and it was inevitable that, in some way, we'd all get caught like a deer in the headlights. Perhaps we just underestimated the severity of the impact that a pandemic such as COVID-19 could have on our societies. Or did we just miss the warning signs?

When we were starting to respond to the first waves of the pandemic, Bill Gates's 2015 TED Talk 'The next outbreak? We're not ready' was widely shared across social media platforms.

Back in 2015, Bill Gates suggested that '...if anything kills over ten million people in the next few decades, it's most likely to be a highly infectious virus, rather than a war.' Part of the reason, he pointed out, is that we've invested very little in a system to stop a pandemic. Among other things, Gates recommended that we do simulations so we could identify the holes in our systems to ensure that we wouldn't get caught off guard.

Soon, we'll be listening to the critics who, with the benefit of hind-sight, will tell us what our leaders should have done better, how they could have reacted faster or how they should have taken a more balanced approach. And though those criticisms might be valid, they'll offer little utility to those who have had to pay a hefty price.

But imagine if our leaders had had the opportunity to fail before, while dealing with a similar scenario. Picture a situation where they had the opportunity to see the consequences of their decisions on a variety of stakeholder groups. Imagine they already had the opportunity to learn from their mistakes. Again, the flight simula-tor is the perfect metaphor. Imagine we all had the opportunity to spend more time practising a safe landing, for that unlikely event where the engines fail.

ADAPTABILITY SKILLS

I love the idea that adaptability is a form of intelligence that can be tested, measured and improved. In her 2019 TED Talk, Natalie Fratto speaks about the three tricks she uses to assess someone's adaptability – how well a person reacts to the inevitability of change. To determine a person's adaptability quotient (AQ), she looks for three things – the person's inclination to ask 'what if' questions, signs of unlearning and the person's willingness to live in a state of constant seeking.

By asking 'what if' questions, we force our brains to simulate. Natalie Fratto claims that a person's ability to picture multiple scenarios, or possible versions of the future, says a lot about their adaptive intel-ligence. Rather than testing how we take in and retain information, like an IQ test, this tests a person's ability to 'manipulate information, given a constraint, to achieve a specific goal'.

Similarly, a simulation exercise asks us to weigh up options that will take us down different paths. Not only do we get to consider several versions of a possible future, but we also get immediate feedback and insight into the opportunities, risks and trade-offs of alternative choices.

Natalie Fratto claims that people with strong adaptive intelligence are active unlearners. They seek to challenge what they presume to already know.

But unlearning doesn't come naturally; it is something we need to develop. There are countless examples of people finding better ways to do things, but at first, our natural impulse is to reject the new approach. It's called the status quo bias. We prefer to stick to our reference point (the status quo) and perceive any change from this reference point as a loss. My favourite example is the Fosbury Flop, named after Dick Fosbury, who was the first Olympian to do the high jump over the bar backwards and headfirst. His competition responded with: *That may work for him, but it won't work for us*. Today, we can't imagine an Olympian attempting the high jump any other way. How would you respond in a similar situation? How long until you would be willing to give up the scissor kick that you've been practising for years?

It's a useful metaphor to help us understand our reluctance to change. We might be aware that teams and organisations around the world are figuring out ways of working that are more suited to the highly networked world that we live in today. Yet, our natural impulse is to stick with what we know and what we are good at. A new approach might feel much like attempting the Fosbury Flop for the first time. Our old ways will probably still yield better results today. A new approach takes patience and practice.

Finally, Fratto argues that, collectively, all of us tend to overvalue exploitation and focus too little on exploration. What that means is that our attention tends to be drawn to exploiting opportunities that are in front of us and already commercially successful. We pay less attention to the less quantifiable, future-focused ideas.

What are the behaviours that are rewarded and incentivised in your business? My experience tells me that our key performance indicators (KPIs) typically measure and reward activities that make the numbers today, not what might make the numbers in the future. Imagine, instead of sales targets, we had value-creation targets. What might those look like? And how would that change the way we prioritise our activities?

Fratto suggests that we should never fall too far in love with our wins, but should remain in a state of constant seeking. The story she uses is the perfect analogy (here is an extract from the transcript):

> In the year 2000, a man finagled his way into a meeting with John Antioco, the CEO of Blockbuster, and proposed a partnership to manage Blockbuster's fledgling online business. The CEO, John, laughed him out of the room, saying, 'I have millions of existing customers and thousands of successful retail stores. I really need to focus on the money.'

> The other man in the meeting, however, turned out to be Reed Hastings, the CEO of Netflix. In 2018, Netflix brought in 15.8 billion dollars, while Blockbuster filed for bankruptcy in 2010, directly ten years after that meeting.

We need to develop our adaptability skills so we can navigate our way through uncertainty, despite a lack of reference points. We need to be able to imagine a set of plausible futures and pressure test our strategies against those scenarios. Regardless whether we are talking about opportunities or risks, the same principles apply.

ERA OF UNCERTAINTY

The acronym VUCA (used to describe conditions of volatility, uncertainty, complexity and ambiguity) has been around since 1987, and for over thirty years we've been acutely aware that being able to operate in a VUCA world is a critical part of strategic leadership. However, we often still find ourselves woefully underprepared for risk events that we can predict with a reasonable level of certainty. The ongoing inaction on climate change is a great example. Remember the movie *An Inconvenient Truth*? It was released in 2006, almost fifteen years ago, and, still, we have many businesses and governments dragging their feet and in denial about the urgency for action.

It reminds me of Natalie Fratto's Blockbuster example, with the CEO laughing Reed Hastings out of the room, because he had to focus on the money. In the same way, we have country leaders laughing climate scientists out the room because they need to focus on the economy. No one is arguing that commercial imperatives or healthy economies aren't important! We need healthy businesses while, at the same time, we need to be able to see around corners and be prepared for what's next. It's not either/or; it's both/and – and that requires adaptability skills.

Climate change and COVID-19 are useful examples in that all of us can relate to them in some way. But there are, of course, thousands of other risk events that happen in our businesses every day. The scale might be smaller, but when they are part of our world, they can be just as devastating – even though the rest of the world pays little attention.

Sometimes, we can anticipate risks and put in place measures to mitigate them or minimise consequences. But guarding against all risks would be prohibitively expensive, so we need to weigh up the likelihood of a risk event occurring against the severity of that event. With increasing levels of uncertainty, it becomes increasingly difficult to have a systems response to every risk. When events hit without warning, we will always need to rely on our people's judgement and their swift response.

In the CEB article 'Reducing Risk Management's Organizational Drag', the authors argue that 'risk management that focuses too much on process and systems – but not enough on enabling better, more proactive risk decision making by employees – overlooks that business risks are magnified or minimized based on human behaviour and judgment.'

'The ability to manage risks,' they conclude, 'must become an essential leadership competency – on par with (and integral to) executing a strategy, launching a new product, and leading an effective team.'

We can't practise while we're in crisis. We need to make sure we give people opportunities to practise when we can afford to take time to prepare.

THE VALUE OF PREPAREDNESS

The relevant simulation experience, done right, can help us be better prepared for an uncertain future. Using simulations and risk-free scenarios will heighten our ability to sense, shape and adapt to what lies ahead. They allow us to identify blind spots and learn from mistakes. Through practice, we can develop the capabilities that will allow us to deal with the unexpected and be confident and resourceful enough to course-correct on the spot.

It is not uncommon that we fail to recognise the value of preparedness. When we are prepared, problems are invisible. Had we been prepared for COVID-19, the virus might not have made it out of Wuhan. Had that been the case, most of us would have been none the wiser about the bullet we would have dodged. Preparedness is everything, even if it is invisible. Preparedness could have saved Blockbuster from bankruptcy or avoided a pandemic. And while we might not be able to predict what the future holds, we can develop our adaptability potential. We can practise; we can simulate.

METHOD – FINAL THOUGHTS

The reason we choose business simulations or experiential learning methodologies for strategy education is that they allow people to deeply engage with the topic in a way that is meaningful to them, as individuals.

The alternative is to simply *tell* people about the strategy. But simply telling people might not be enough if we want people to remember, understand or know how to translate strategy for their teams.

Creating a business simulation experience takes time and effort. However, if the message we are conveying is important, then we want to give people an opportunity to engage with it, in a way that is fun and engaging! We want to ensure learners can engage with *what if* questions that relate to *their* world. They need an opportunity to unlearn the behaviours that are holding *them* back.

If we want people to be good at executing strategy, we need to create an environment in which people are free to tackle strategic challenges that are relevant to them, in their area of influence.

PART 2

MESSAGE

IN THE CONTEXT OF BUSINESS SIMULATIONS, MESSAGE IS about crafting a narrative that allows your people to engage with your strategy in a way that is relevant to them, as individuals. But to be able to speak about that, I would first need to learn more about *your* strategy. And creating a simulation experience that is a good fit will typically require several conversations with you, and with other leaders in your organisation. When it comes to developing business simulations, the level of customisation and co-creation is entirely up to you.

The purpose of this section is aimed at sharing examples. Examples of different types of *messages* we might be able to script into a simulation experience. Perhaps these examples will spark some ideas that help you imagine a simulation experience that you might want to create for your teams.

The examples I share are based on existing solutions – I call them the *Coffee Shop*, *Secure-O-Tech* and *OzSwell* Simulations. These solutions were created to address the business challenges discussed in

Chapter 2. On occasion, you will hear me referring to the *alignment & evolution* model (and before reading the next chapters, perhaps you'll find it useful to familiarise yourself with that model again — back on page 27).

The idea is to give you an insight into what a simulation challenge might look like for different audiences and, consequently, the skill-sets we might need to develop. It would be possible to run any of these sample simulations without customisation. However, it is best to think of them as existing platforms that can be fully customised based on your business model or strategy.

Each of these simulation experiences can be delivered face to face or virtually. A typical event will run for one to two days. The virtual sessions will take up a similar amount of time, but they are usually delivered in bite-sized chunks, over a period of two to three weeks.

PERSPECTIVE

You only have one strategy for your organisation, but how people engage with it will differ depending on their level of seniority or their day-to-day roles. Defining the audience is going to be critical to creating the *'right'* simulation experience. Our challenge for business might be the same, but it plays out differently depending on where people are on their journey as leaders. Our simulation challenge needs to meet people where they are at.

Figure 5: A helicopter perspective

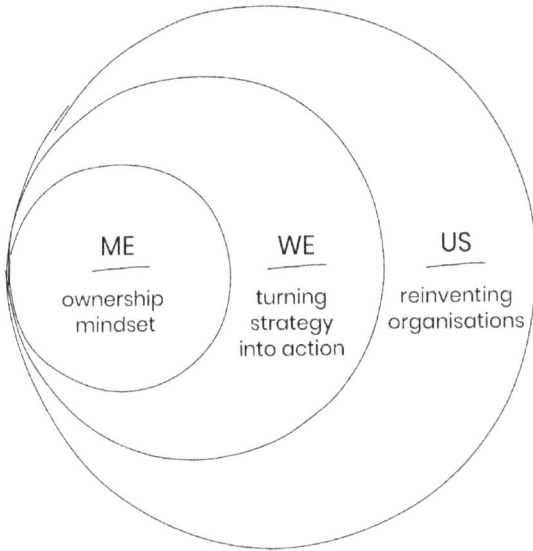

When we talk about business simulations, we often refer to the experience as taking a helicopter perspective. The world looks quite different from up above, and the higher we climb the broader our field of vision becomes. Our business simulation allows us to see our business from this elevated perspective. As our metaphorical helicopter rises, we will initially just see our business unit. As we climb, we get to see the entire business. Climb even further and we will see how our business connects with other businesses, the community and the economy at large.

In a similar way, our perspective changes depending on the level of seniority from which we operate. The more senior we get, the broader the perspective we need to take. And the bigger the ramifications of our actions. We need to customise our simulation narrative in a way that aligns with the perspective of our audience.

If the storyline is too far removed from our reality, the simulation might be fun, but it will not lead to those 'aha' moments that ultimately inspire behavioural change.

The model shown in Figure 5 is an attempt at illustrating these three perspectives. These perspectives also make up the following three chapters.

HOW TO READ THE PART 2 CHAPTERS

If you have a particular audience in mind for your simulation solution, you might want to focus on the chapter that is most relevant to them, and just skim the others.

> The business challenge: How do we evolve to meet the demands of an uncertain environment? How do we ensure alignment across strategy, people and systems?

Here is a brief overview of the target audience and the perspectives that the following chapters will address.

Developing an **Ownership Mindset** is an experience that is targeted at individuals who are new to leading projects, initiatives or small teams (e.g. frontline managers or project leaders). The focus is on the individual – **ME** – and ensuring the individual has the skillset to take complete ownership of a project or problem.

The **Turning Strategy into Action** experience is targeted

at individuals who lead teams in large organisations (e.g. regional managers or functional leaders). They are responsible for effective strategy execution in their realm of influence. The focus is on teams – **WE** – and ensuring leaders have the skillsets needed to coordinate efforts and allocate resources for multiple individuals or teams.

Reinventing Organisations is a simulation experience targeted at senior and executive leaders who have the authority to set strategy for their business, division, function or team. The focus is on the community at large and the impact that the decisions we make in business have on all of – **US** – today and into the future.

The following chapters deal primarily with the strategy challenges our organisations are facing, and what skillsets our simulation solutions can help us build.

I am aware that, when it comes to simulations, getting to see the simulation tool and all the collateral that make up the experience is just as important as talking about business challenges. You might even be keen to make some of your own decisions in the simulation tool and have a play!

The only way to do that is by experiencing a demo session. If that sounds interesting to you, have a look at the *Connect with Me* section at the back of the book. I would love to welcome you to a webcast or a live demo event.

For now, think about your audience, pick your chapter and let's explore some of the business challenges that our simulation solutions can help us address...

DEVELOPING AN OWNERSHIP MINDSET

IMAGINE YOU ARE NEW TO THE WORLD OF BUSINESS, CURIOUS about how your organisation creates value, makes money and coordinates the efforts of its people. When we are hired into a large organisation that has been around for decades, it can be difficult to make sense of everything that is going on. Scale brings with it all manners of complexity. How do we make sense of the bigger picture when we are separated into functional silos and asked to focus on just a specific task? In such a structure, it's not uncommon to feel like a cog in a wheel and to simply do what's been asked.

Our key performance indicators (KPIs) are supposed to somehow guide us and tell us whether or not we're doing a good job. But if all we are doing is chasing metrics, it can be difficult to have a deeper sense of purpose, to understand the *why* behind our actions.

What we need is a learning experience that helps us understand the big picture: a simpler business and an opportunity to take full accountability for all decision making.

*What if we could learn the way our founding
entrepreneurs did? What if we can?*

The *Ownership Mindset* experience is targeted at individuals who are new to business or who lead projects or teams on the frontline. They are responsible for coordination and outcomes of specific projects or initiatives. The simulation experience is an opportunity for learners to take full accountability for the start-up and the operations of a small, simulated business.

Let's put ourselves in the shoes of the learner and explore how a simulation experience may help us develop an ownership mindset.

If we're entrepreneurs starting a new business, we typically start small. We are involved in all aspects of our small business and are close to everything. We have a direct relationship with our suppliers. We are involved in the manufacture of our product. We post on social media and position our product to the world. We sell, we invoice and we celebrate every time we can bank a few dollars. At the beginning, our start-up venture is strapped for cash! We can't afford help, so we need to learn everything there is to know about all aspects of our business. Finance, production, sales, accounting – you name it, we've got to be across it all. The start-up phase is an exciting learning experience for any entrepreneur!

Now, put yourself in those shoes. Imagine *YOU* decided to become a small business owner. What would it be like? Perhaps it is something you've considered before, but you decided the risk is too high. But what if you had the opportunity to practise, without the risk? A simulated business rather than a real one?

Most people get a little bit excited about the prospect of running a business of their own, or even just by the prospect of having more autonomy. Our simulation allows us to get a real sense of what it might be like to have complete ownership of and responsibility for a business and its people. It challenges our assumptions, it questions our business savvy and it allows us to strategise and choose how to play. Competitors will challenge us, unexpected events will shake things up, but the choice of how to respond is entirely up to us.

We get to put our assumptions to the test, making bold moves that will result in success or maybe failure. Either way, we will learn from our mistakes. Regardless of whether we win or lose, we will get to see what good looks like. We will hone our strategy, business acumen and commercial skills, skills that we'll be able to leverage back in the real world.

So, first, we create a scenario...

THE COFFEE SHOP SIMULATION

Imagine you had the opportunity to start your own coffee shop, from scratch. What would you need to know about business to ensure you are set up for success?

As a participant of the Coffee Shop Simulation, you receive a case study that gives you all the background information you need prior to embarking on your simulation adventure. In it you find information about the market, about competitors and about different customer segments and their buying preferences. You need to choose a location, analyse data, consider options and contemplate different strategic approaches.

The Coffee Shop Simulation is an opportunity for you to take a holistic, end-to-end approach to decision making. How will you fund your business? What kind of investments will you make? And how will you manage day-to-day operations?

ENTREPRENEURIAL LEADERS

How good does it feel to work with people who truly OWN their job? I used to work with a colleague called Sam, who would thrive when she was given a difficult task. She would quickly grasp what needed to get done, get creative, energise the team and make magic happen. You would often hear colleagues say, 'If only we had ten of her...'

The thing that set her apart was her ownership mindset. She didn't just do her job – she owned it. It's easy to identify people who have this mindset – they're the people everyone wants on their team. They're so full of initiative that it spreads to others around them. You don't pick them just for their technical skill, but because of their mindset. It's like choosing a builder to complete renovations on your home; you're probably more interested in good referrals (will they own it?), rather than technical qualifications (can they do it?).

In the *Harvard Business Review* article 'Hiring an Entrepreneurial Leader', Timothy Butler argues that leaders with an entrepreneurial mindset have three qualities that set them apart:

1. They take complete ownership of a venture or problem;
2. They are more motivated as uncertainty increases; and
3. They have a remarkable ability to persuade others to follow their course of action.

These certainly sound like the qualities displayed by Sam. They're the qualities that gave her team confidence that their project would be successful.

However, ownership mindset is not some magical talent that is only bestowed on the few. It is something that is within all of us. It's just, often, fear of failure can hold us back from exploring that potential.

Everyone possesses the qualities above – they just come to the fore when we are presented with challenges that leave us no other choice but to step up. We don't develop these qualities by reading textbooks. We develop them through experimentation and trial and error.

What we need are the skills, the confidence and the mindset – and all of these can be practised.

RESPONSIBILITY TO THE EDGES

Most organisations are busy going through some form of transformation in which they are establishing ways of working that are better suited to our fast-changing, interconnected world. Not only do our company CEOs need to be able to adapt strategy in the moment, we also need to be able to react to changes quickly on the frontline. Traditional structures where thinking happens at the top and execution happens at the bottom are too slow to deal with changing circumstances in real time.

We need frontline leaders who can lead, own and execute strategy. What's needed is a willingness to take ownership of a problem and rise to the challenge of solving it. Like the kind of people that raise their hands when volunteers are needed. They are not afraid to get their hands dirty; they understand the job to be done, and accountability comes from within.

The *alignment & evolution* model discussed in Chapter 2 suggests that fast-changing environments require that our people be empowered, that they can act with autonomy.

Developing an ownership mindset is about helping people make the shift *above the line* on the *people* dimension. To feel comfortable in this space, leaders need the following three things:

- We need to develop the **mindset** where we can be trusted to take ownership of our projects.
- We need to understand the **business fundamentals**. It is the foundation on which everything else rests.
- We need to understand **value creation** in the context of the whole of the business and how our customers' perception of value is constantly shifting.

LEADERSHIP ABOVE THE LINE

Let's take a more detailed look at the three things leaders need to cultivate to own the shift:

MINDSET

When we are hired into a large corporation, with hundreds or thousands of people, it can be difficult to get a sense of how different parts of the business work together to create value. Typically, we are hired for a specific job that requires us to focus on just one tiny piece of an enormous puzzle. We're immediately thrown into the action of everyday operations. We get given a set of problems and a list of targets we're expected to hit, and off we go – immediately consumed by the busyness of stuff.

The journey looks different for an entrepreneur starting a new business – no one tells them what to do or where to focus. Entrepreneurs don't have all the answers they need when they dive headfirst into their new venture. Perhaps they think they do, but they soon realise that their plan is fraught with flawed assumptions. The carefully plotted path ends up taking twists and turns that no one could have foreseen. What sets entrepreneurs apart from everyone else is not some magical ability – it's that they dare to take the leap, for better or worse. Regardless of the outcome, the learning is tremendous. We can't all afford to take big risks, but we can attempt to replicate a similar learning journey in an environment that's not quite so perilous.

To develop an ownership mindset, we don't need to simulate a massive organisation. We can strip back all the layers until we get back to basics – back to where it all started.

We get to start from a blank canvas, where we can learn the way our founders did.

We get the chance to be across every decision, soak up the learning and make our own rookie mistakes.

Regardless of the size, all businesses operate on the same basic principles. We need to make the same types of decisions – financing, investing and operating. The same accounting principles apply. We have a profit and loss statement, a balance sheet and a cash flow statement. And we need to create value and somehow charge for that value. So, what if we start with the basics? What does it take to run a successful business?

An ownership mindset is not about knowing, but rather about being comfortable with learning through a process of experimentation with the unknown. By removing the fear of failure, it is easy for us to adopt what Psychology Professor Carol Dweck refers to as a *growth mindset* – the belief that most of our basic abilities can be developed through dedication and hard work. Brains and talent are just the starting point.

There is no 'correct' way to approach the challenge. We need to make do with the information we have and figure out the rest. We learn by doing.

BUSINESS FUNDAMENTALS

When we start our simulation adventure, we're armed with nothing but a case study and a bit of background information. We'll find some interesting market stats and perhaps a bit of info about our competitors, but it is hardly enough to help us make great decisions. How much money are we going to need? And where are we going to get it?

Despite our uncertainty, we start to enter a few of our decisions into our simulation tool. We start by making initial financing and investment decisions and we see a *balance sheet* start to populate. As we start making operational decisions, we see a *profit and loss statement* start to build. Financial ratios start to appear on the simulation dashboard with acronyms like ROA, EBITDA and EVA. How do we make sense of the data, the jargon and the unfamiliar acronyms?

We don't all need finance degrees to understand how the business makes money. But we do need a solid understanding of the business fundamentals to be able to make good business decisions. Simulations are not necessarily designed to teach disciplines such as finance, but as part of the experience, we gain just the right amount of financial know-how to ensure we have the basic blocks on which we can build.

We learn to read financial statements because it serves a purpose. We need to be able to make sense of the numbers so they can help guide our decision making. We want to know why rival teams have outperformed us. We scrutinise our financial statements looking for answers. Did we spend too much? Did we not charge enough? Are we utilising our assets efficiently?

When financial statements tell *OUR* story, they become a lot more interesting than the random-company annual financials that you find in your typical finance textbook. When knowledge has direct applicability, we are thirsty for it! We are eager to listen to the theory because it gives us the answers we seek.

VALUE CREATION

Value creation is at the heart of what we do in business. If we don't create value, customers don't buy. And when we're not selling, we can't survive. Simple as that.

What is less clear is the concept of value itself. How do we quantify or measure it? How much should we be charging? By taking small bets, innovating, changing pricing and adding or removing features, we get to collect feedback from the market and discover how different customer segments behave. We're continuously testing and exploring and trying new things. And so are our competitors.

We need to be able to listen, able to innovate and able to commercialise our ideas. The playing field is never static and falling behind could put an end to the business. We need to be good at playing this game. All the more reason to practise.

If we take the customer perspective, we know that our perception of value is always shifting, depending on what is available. Take the value of a box of matches, for example – extremely valuable in the wilderness; less so in urban life. Value is not necessarily about the product itself, but about the problem it helps us solve.

In our sim-world, we get to create our own value propositions. Whether it is the quality of our coffee beans or the skill level of the baristas we hire. In this world, we get to make all the choices. And it's not about being right or wrong. It is about experimenting with the concept of value creation and differentiation. It's about making small bets, collecting feedback and making adjustments as we go.

We get to learn about strategy concepts, like Clayton Christensen's *Jobs-to-Be-Done* or the *Strategy Canvas* developed by professors W. Chan Kim and Renee Mauborgne. But it is not about the theoretical discussions. These are concepts that can be immediately applied to the challenge we're immersed in. These are tools we can use to help us understand how to prioritise and differentiate.

When we find better ways to solve existing problems, we create uncontested market spaces. And uncontested market spaces allow us to define the rules of the game. We get to lead, rather than follow. And reap the rewards that come with it. It is only through curiosity and experimentation that we can push the boundaries of possibility.

LEARNING LIKE ENTREPRENEURS

The joy of being able to operate with autonomy is the freedom that comes with being able to make our own choices. In business environments shaped by fast-paced change, we need experiences that allow us to be comfortable with the business fundamentals. We need a place where we can practise making considered commercial choices. We need to understand the impact our decisions have on the wider system and the multitude of stakeholders we serve. We need to develop an intuitive understanding of how the business creates value and how we continually need to find new ways to solve problems for customers. We need the confidence to put forward our ideas, get buy-in from others and make things happen.

If the future demands increased levels of autonomy and more accountability on the frontline, we need to learn the way entrepreneurs do.

A simulated start-up venture is a great place to start!

FIND OUT MORE

The *Coffee Shop Simulation* is an existing simulation platform that is a great tool for helping people develop their business acumen and strategic thinking. Though the simulation narrative is about starting a business, it is not targeted at people that want to start a business of their own. Rather, its purpose is to help people who work in large businesses understand how business works – people who might never otherwise have the opportunity to learn about business the way that entrepreneurs do.

The *Coffee Shop Simulation* is just an example of a platform that helps learners develop these kinds of skillsets. Have a look at the *Connect with Me* section for more information on this specific solution.

TURNING STRATEGY INTO ACTION

WHEN WE WORK IN LARGE BUSINESSES, WE COME TOGETHER to achieve something bigger than ourselves, something we cannot achieve on our own. When we lead, it is no longer just about us as individuals – our skillset, our mindset and our ideas.

We need to make the shift from ME to WE.

The *Turning Strategy into Action* experience is targeted at individuals who lead teams in large organisations (e.g. regional managers or functional leaders). They are responsible for effective strategy execution in their realm of influence. The simulation experience allows them to explore and experiment with different approaches. How will they deliver the best results? Are their efforts aligned with the overall strategy and the organisation's purpose?

Let's put ourselves in the shoes of the learner and explore how a simulation experience can help us turn strategy into action.

Many of us aspire to take on leadership or management roles. We're keen to be the person that calls the shots, controls the resources and gets to set the direction for the group. Not to mention the privileges. Better status, more power and increased pay. Why wouldn't we want to strive for that?

But not everyone who aspires to climb the ranks has a genuine interest in leading others. While being a boss might give us rank or status, being a leader is about acting in service to others.

'A boss has the title. A leader has the people.'
– SIMON SINEK

So, what makes a good leader? What is it that our organisation asks of us? And are we prepared for the challenges that lie ahead?

The shift from *ME* to *WE* requires us to evolve into the next level of our leadership. Our role is to manage and coordinate the efforts of our teams. Their success is our success. How do we ensure alignment? How do we ensure we prioritise the right actions and get things done? How do we allocate resources? How do we lead others and enable them to do their best work?

Learning from mistakes in the real world can be tricky. It's not always clear whether the decisions we make are good or bad. Sometimes, we do not get to see the consequences of our decisions, or it can take months, even years, before we learn from feedback.

Furthermore, the real world does not always provide us with comparative data. Perhaps different assumptions would have led to better outcomes.

'Until you make the unconscious conscious, it will direct your life and you will call it fate.'

– CARL JUNG

The simulated world allows us to remove some of the real-world learning impediments. We get to learn from immediate feedback and can compare our choices against those of our peers. We get to uncover our assumptions and discuss them in an environment that is risk-free. If some of the assumptions we are making are flawed, this is the environment where we want to uncover them.

In the simulated world, we are free to challenge the status quo and test new ideas. We are not bound by existing processes or procedures, and we are free to remove or change the systems that do not serve us. What changes will we make? Time to stop guessing and start testing!

Let's look at a relevant simulation scenario...

THE SECURE-O-TECH SIMULATION

Imagine you (and your simulation team) are hired as functional/divisional leaders of a regional security company called Secure-O-Tech. Picture a company with several divisions, each with their own challenges, ideas and ambitions.

As a participating team, you receive a case study with background information about the company. It is a company that is, of course, fictitious, but the stories and challenges are informed by interviews, literature reviews, case studies and other real-world data. The narrative is carefully crafted to ensure it is relevant to you and your leadership challenges.

The case study sets the scene. You and your team get an insight into the company's history and financial performance. It highlights current issues such as declining growth, quality issues and infighting. The business has been under pressure due to digital disruption and increased regulatory requirements.

These challenges have brought about a leadership change for Secure-O-Tech. Into the role of CEO steps an inspiring and visionary leader. She is keen to transition the organisation from its traditional past to a cyber-security-focused and digital future.

The CEO is a purpose-led leader who believes that every person has the right to feel safe, in both the physical and virtual world. Most people in the organisation are inspired by her energy and vision for the future. However, many of the company's leaders are holding on to the status quo, unwilling to turn away from what they know.

Your job is to support your visionary leader. She has painted a picture of the future. Your role is to help turn that dream into reality.

The simulation exercise is an opportunity for you and your team to consider possibilities and discuss ideas, without having to navigate some of the complexities of the real world. You are free to make things simpler, remove red-tape and put an end to the business's stifling, bureaucratic ways. You are able to make operational decisions and launch initiatives to guide your teams in a new direction. You need to deal with scenarios that require you to set the course. Your choices, your investments and your behaviours set the tone for the culture you are trying to create.

Will the direction be clear? Will you be consistent? Aligned? And future ready?

Let's explore...

IDEAS INTO ACTION

Do you ever wish you were an inventor? Maybe your inner voice sometimes says, 'If this were my company, I'd be able to create a better product, fix this issue, offer better service, contribute to a better planet.' What amazing ideas are buried in your mind and left invisible to the world?

As customers, we're often frustrated by things that don't work. We've all had ideas about how products or services can be improved.

I remember not being able to sleep on a sixteen-hour, long-haul flight because I was squashed next to someone who had taken control of the armrest. Wide awake and with an elbow jutting into my ribcage, I had a lot of time to ponder alternative ways of arranging the seating. How difficult would it be to create an economy-class seat that has separate armrests or maybe a divider? What if the seats were slightly offset so you didn't need to spend hours in an armrest-domination battle?

But apart from complaining, we feel powerless and simply accept the inconvenience – we've booked economy, after all.

I'm sure that, collectively, economy-class travellers around the world have spent millions of hours dreaming up better seating arrangements. But we'll probably never do anything with our ideas. And ideas that cannot be turned into action are ultimately worthless.

Turning ideas into action is hard! Genius is not just in the ideas, it's in the ability to follow through. Interestingly, Albert Einstein is quoted as saying, 'It's not that I'm so smart, I just stay with problems longer.'

Our ability to follow through on ideas is what is critical to success, especially in an environment of uncertainty. Survey findings suggest that approximately two-thirds of strategies are not successfully implemented. Sounds like a high number, but it shouldn't be too surprising given that execution is the hard part.

Strategy is the idea; execution is turning that idea into action. If we want to make a difference, we must be good at doing.

Business simulations give us a platform that allows leaders to experiment with execution challenges. In the simulated world, we have the authority to make changes as we see fit. By testing ideas, making mistakes, taking on feedback and through open discussion in a safe space, we get to develop an intuitive understanding of what it means to turn strategy into action.

LEADING IN COMPLEXITY

When we join an organisation, we inherit structures, policies and systems that have been created by those who came before us. They have become part of the fabric of our organisation. But what are the assumptions that informed the choices that our predecessors made? What if the existing systems were okay during their time, but are now outdated, too slow for our tech-driven world?

In his book *Brave New Work*, Aaron Dignan reminds us that the way we work is completely made up. We should be grateful for the inherited systems and processes that serve us, while knowing that we can change the rest.

Our *alignment & evolution* model suggests that, from a systems perspective, we can either operate *below the line* – a complicated systems approach, characterised by control and efficiency, or *above the line* – a complex systems approach, characterised by connection and relationships. Let us define the two concepts in a little more detail.

A **complicated system** is a causal system – meaning that we can predict what it is going to do. It might be made up of millions of components, but the parts within the system interact in highly predictable ways. An engine, a watch and a production line are good examples. The parts of the system interact with each other in a cause-and-effect relationship. If our engine is broken, we can find the faulty part, replace it and the problem is solved.

A **complex system**, on the other hand, is dynamic. Effect is rarely proportional to cause. Complex systems are history-dependent, self-organising, adaptive and counterintuitive. Examples are the weather, traffic and the internet. Even though we can make predictions about what our complex system is likely to do, we cannot control it.

> Aaron Dignan offers a practical metaphor to help us understand how the different assumptions we make about our world can lead to very different systems solutions. The metaphor he uses is a road intersection. The problem – how do we manage the intersection for maximum flow of traffic,

without cars crashing into each other? This is how Dignan explains the assumptions behind two popular solutions to the problem.

A signal-controlled intersection is a complicated systems approach to the problem. The assumptions – people need to be told what to do; we need a plan for every possible scenario; we need elaborate rules and technology to optimise traffic flow.

A roundabout is a complex systems approach to the problem. The assumptions – people can be trusted to use their own judgement; simple rules and agreements are all the guidance we need to manage complex problems; social coordination will be sufficient to handle a wide range of scenarios.

The point of the story is not to make a case for the best type of road intersection, but rather to highlight that our systems approach needs to be aligned with the strategy we are pursuing. If we translate the metaphor for our organisations, we might conclude that predictable tasks, like manufacturing, might be best served with a complicated systems approach that ensures consistency, quality and efficiency. If we operate in unpredictable environments, however, we need systems that allow us to respond to the situation at hand.

The *Turning Strategy into Action* simulation is about honing our ability to lead *above the line* on the systems dimension. To operate effectively in this space, leaders need to be able to do the following three things:

- **Act with clarity** – Create the guiding principles to ensure we are all working towards a common purpose.

- **Engage with curiosity** – Ensure we are able to listen and act on signals of change.
- **Lead with courage** – Create an environment where people can do the best work of their lives, while allowing for adaptability.

THE RIGHT OPERATING SYSTEM

Just like we use maps to help us navigate cities, we can use simulations to help us understand how to navigate complex businesses. As discussed, simulations are simplifications of reality designed to promote understanding. They help us understand how things connect and how small changes to one part of the system influence other parts.

ACT WITH CLARITY

The CEO has shared her vision. It is fresh, ambitious and exciting. We're inspired; now what?

The role of the CEO is to create a vision – to share the dream. The role of operational leaders is to operationalise the vision – to turn vision into reality. A well-articulated vision of the future can inspire us, but, ultimately, impact comes from action.

The authors of *Execution – The Discipline of Getting Things Done* caution that we should not confuse execution with tactics. Instead, we should think of execution as a discipline and a system. If it is our job to turn a vision into reality, we need to ensure that the policies and procedures that we have inherited are not standing in the way of our execution capability.

> *'We do not rise to the level of our goals. We fall to the level of our systems.'*
> — JAMES CLEAR

We need to ensure that we create the enabling conditions so that our teams can do the best work of their lives. We need to evaluate our systems and processes, ensuring that the underlying assumptions are aligned with our strategy.

At the heart of it all, our challenge is this:

The teams we lead all have great ideas, but we need to share scarce resources.

This puts us in a position where we need to deal with trade-offs. Whose ideas get the necessary funding and whose ideas are sidelined? We need to maximise value creation with limited resources, while simultaneously ensuring fairness, engagement and motivation. Our job as an operational leader is to ensure we have the systems in place that create clarity and set the guiding principles for our teams.

In complex environments, we don't know where the best ideas will come from. We need to encourage our teams to evolve, and continuously seek new ways of working and/or creating value. To be able to act with agility, we need simple guiding principles that allow us to use our own judgement so that we can move forward immediately.

Jason Fried and David Heinemeier Hansson, authors of *Rework*, argue that we do not create a culture, but rather that culture is a byproduct of consistent behaviours. The choices we make in our simulated environment are signposts for the behaviours we encourage or tolerate. How we respond to unexpected events says a lot about the type of organisation that we are building. To lead effectively in complex environments, we need to understand that all elements of our system are held together by relationships. In our simulated world, we get to test whether the behaviours we are encouraging are aligned with the future we seek to build.

ENGAGE WITH CURIOSITY

When was the last time you switched from an established brand or 'trusted' provider? How bad did things have to get before you felt compelled to switch?

We often hear the phrase 'digital disruption', and the word 'digital' seems to suggest that companies with innovative new technologies are stealing our customers, with technology as the source of the disruption. It turns out that most disruption events can be tied to finding better ways to serve, rather than innovative new technologies. Disruptors typically leverage technology that is freely available.

In his book *Unlocking the Customer Value Chain*, Thales Teixeira argues that digital technologies have made it possible to decouple parts of the customer value chain. That means that disruptors can focus on improving just selected elements of the overall customer experience. They turn something that is difficult, annoying or costly into something that is simpler, quicker and cheaper. And while businesses may leverage technology to create better experiences, it is the experience itself that drives customer behaviour.

When we work in large organisations that are split into functional silos, we can lose sight of the end-to-end customer experience. A *Harvard Business Review* article claims that 'crafting a great

customer experience requires enormous amounts of collaboration...
in many cases marketing, product design, customer services, sales,
advertising, and retail partners must all be working in concert to
create even a single touchpoint.'

If, as a business, value creation is what we do, then we're in a dangerous place when other players are better at the value-creation
game. For many traditional businesses, the threat of disruption is
very real. But the disruptors aren't necessarily reinventing the wheel;
they're simply finding better ways to solve problems.

Our simulated world allows us to experiment, test and learn. We
invest in technology, systems and big data to ensure we gather the
information we need. But gathering information is not sufficient. We
need to learn how to use and interpret it. I like Clayton M. Christensen's take on this, and his theory on *Customers' Jobs-to-Be-Done*.
Rather than looking at things from our perspective and adding
features to our products that we think are valuable, Christiansen
argues that we need to be clear on what the problem is that we
are solving. A concept that is beautifully summed up in this quote:

> *'People don't want to buy a quarter-inch drill.*
> *They want a quarter-inch hole.'*
>
> – THEODORE LEVITT

We need to be clear on the problem we are solving for our customers and create enabling systems that allow our teams to act on that
information. If we want our organisations to be more adaptive, we
need the skillsets that allow us to listen and act on signals of change.
Because customers' perception of value is constantly shifting, we
need to be in a state of constant seeking.

LEAD WITH COURAGE

Occasionally in life we have the privilege of being mentored by someone whom we personally consider to be a great leader. Who are the individuals that had the greatest influence on your career or personal development? What are some of the characteristics that set them apart from the rest?

We remember these leaders, mentors and teachers not because they were able to give us the right answers, but because they trusted us to find the right answers. They are the ones that challenged us, pushed us, motivated us and inspired us to grow. We remember them as great leaders because they believed in us!

When we step into a position of authority, we are held accountable for the performance of our team. When we are new to the role, it does not always come easy to us to trust; we fear losing control. Leading in complexity takes courage. Trust is not built overnight. We need to develop an awareness of the assumptions we make about those we lead and the beliefs we hold about human nature. Can people self-manage or do they need to be controlled? Are they trustworthy or undependable?

Taylor's *Scientific Approach to Management* is a classic example of a mindset that assumes that people are inherently lazy and must be coerced, incentivised or told what to do. It is a mindset that can deliver outcomes in predictable environments, but it will not lay the foundations for relationships based on trust.

Unpredictable environments, on the other hand, require empowered individuals that can use their own judgement. The assumption we make when we lead *above the line* is that people are intrinsically motivated and capable of self-direction. The quality of our relationships is key to good performance. In Aaron Dignan's words, *'When it comes to people, you get what you design for.'* Probably a good idea to test our assumptions in a risk-free space.

SYSTEMS-LEVEL STRATEGIC THINKING

To lead effectively in a fast-changing world, we need to understand how complex systems behave, so that we can create the right conditions to allow us to adapt and continually find new ways to achieve our goals.

Our simulation experience gives us an opportunity to test whether our decisions are consistent across strategy, people and systems. We get to compare our decisions against those of our peers and see how different approaches play out both in the short and the long term. It gives us a safe space in which we can play lightly with our decisions – so we can develop an intuitive understanding of what it means to turn strategy into action.

FIND OUT MORE

The *Secure-O-Tech Simulation* is a great tool for helping people to understand the importance of system challenges and to uncover assumptions and discuss these in a risk-free space. It was originally built as a scenario simulation for conferences and has since been built out to include a variety of operational decisions.

As the *Turning Strategy into Action* title suggests, the simulation experience is centred around strategy and, as such, this type of solution should be customised to speak to *your* strategy. The

Secure-O-Tech Simulation provides a useful starting platform that could make the customisation process easier. See the *Connect with Me* section for additional info.

REINVENTING
ORGANISATIONS

IMAGINE YOU ARE PART OF A BUSINESS THAT HAS BEEN SUC-cessful for several decades. And then, all of a sudden, the trusted recipe for success is no longer working. The environment has changed, and the business is no longer able to keep up with low-cost competitors. Perhaps it is a scenario worth testing. How could testing help our decision making today, many years ahead of a possible disruption event?

The narrative of the *Reinventing Organisations* simulation is not necessarily a reflection of our own business, but it is an opportunity for us to step into a crisis scenario. We are forced into a situation where it is adapt or die, which means:

Reinvention is the only way forward.

To do this, we want to adopt a perspective that goes beyond organi-sational boundaries. We view our business as a part of an extended network – part of the economic system and the rules that govern it, part of society and their expectations. We are part of these systems and, as such, we shape and influence what our world looks like. We get to make choices about how we play.

> *Reinventing Organisations* is a simulation experience targeted at senior and executive leaders who have the authority to set strategy for their business, division, function or team. They get to make the 'how to play' choices and determine what success looks like for their area of influence. They are the leaders that make the decisions today that will set the course for the future.

Let's put ourselves in the shoes of the learner and explore how a simulation experience can help us be better prepared for an unknowable future.

We are living in an age where the whole world is in transformation. There are several things happening around us that will fundamentally change what the future looks like for us humans. Whether it is advances in technology or the fact that our planet has a limited capacity – the challenges we face in business are going to be vastly different from the challenges of the past. Finding solutions to some of these problems requires us to play to a new set of rules.

In the *Harvard Business Review* article 'Learning from the Future', author J. Peter Scobolic suggests that *Strategic Foresight* is a theory and practice that offers a way forward. 'Its aim is not to predict the future but rather to imagine multiple futures in creative ways that heighten our ability to sense, shape, and adapt to what happens in the years ahead. Strategic foresight doesn't help us to figure out what to think about the future. It helps us to figure out how to think about it.'

What if you had the authority to make changes to how we create or measure value? What choices would you make today if the success of your initiatives were to be measured several years from now? Why not test some of the assumptions by simulating multiple possible futures?

Let me paint a simulation scenario:

THE OZSWELL SIMULATION

You and your team are appointed as the leadership team of the fictitious company called OzSwell. It is an Australian-owned manufacturer and retailer of surfing apparel. It has a proud history, but over the last decade it has lost its way. The pressure to deliver short-term financial results compelled your predecessors to make decisions that have been detrimental to the organisation's long-term health. This once proud and iconic brand is now struggling to survive in an environment marred by disruption and uncertainly. Your role is to change the course.

As a participant, you receive a case study with information about OzSwell's history and financial performance. You learn about trends and industry challenges. Declining growth and increased pressure on profit margins paint a bleak picture, but it is not all bad news. The community has a strong connection to the brand. It is a brand that people grew up with, and it is close to the heart of the local community. Despite the recent scandals, the company continues to attract talent who are keen to see the brand restored to its former glory.

The simulation exercise allows you and your team to redefine what success looks like for OzSwell. Whether it is customers, employees, shareholders, government or the community – all have a vested interest in the business succeeding. You are given the authority to make the necessary decisions that will ensure the continued long-term survival of the business.

THE RULES OF THE GAME

Here is an observation you might find interesting. In well over a decade of designing and facilitating business simulation experiences, I have hardly ever had anyone question the winning metrics. Winning metrics are usually something like share price or a balanced score card with weighted metrics such as revenue growth, profitability, customer satisfaction and employee engagement. Given that participants get to step into a fictitious role (like CEO), you would think that, occasionally, people would challenge these metrics. Yet, nobody ever does.

Why are we so happy to accept these arbitrary constructs of winning? And when we do, what kind of behaviour does that encourage in the real world? There have been various times in my career that I have been instructed by a senior leader to ensure we make the numbers happen. Whether that meant delaying write-offs or pulling revenues forward, it had to get done! A frenzy of activity to satisfy arbitrary constructs of winning – short-term decision making to boost personal incentives – rather than setting up the business for long-term success. As a team, we were fully aware that these actions would create more pressure for the following year, when higher targets would be set due to our 'great' performance, even though we needed to make up all those revenues we had 'pulled forward'.

We make the numbers we are told to make, because anything

REINVENTING ORGANISATIONS

else would be a career-limiting move. It is just the way the game of business is played. Or is it?

The word strategy has its roots in military history, and it shouldn't be too much of a surprise that a lot of the literature that deals with the topic is about 'winning' or finding ways to beat the competition. When we do an online search for books on *strategy*, we will come across titles such as *Competitive Strategy*, *Playing to Win* and *The Art of War*. Just a glance at these titles might be enough for us to reason that strategy is essentially about defeating our rivals and winning. But there is more to it than that!

When we play *above the line* on the *alignment & evolution* model, strategy is about responsiveness and adaptivity, and less about the competitive nature of the game that is played *below the line*. It is a concept beautifully illustrated in Simon Sinek's book *The Infinite Game*. Sinek bases his findings on an idea first coined by Professor James P. Carse, who claims that we get to choose the rules of how we play – we get to choose to play a finite or an infinite game. The concept is best explained in metaphors.

A *finite game* – is like a football game. There is a clear beginning and an end. How we play is determined by rules we've agreed upon. There is clarity on what winning looks like and when it will be measured.

An *infinite game* – is like education. There is no clear beginning or end. There are no agreed-upon rules. We don't 'win' education. We get to choose how we play. Success is part of the journey – the evolution towards becoming a better version of ourselves. We choose how we show up; when and how we modify the rules is up to us.

When we take a *below-the-line* approach to managing business, it seems rational to measure success as if it is a finite game. Just like goals scored in a football game, we can measure and compare units produced, sales volume, revenue or profit in any given year. And without a doubt, there is value in monitoring our performance.

But our annual financial results don't necessarily translate into superior performance in the infinite game of business. Just like we don't necessarily see the benefits of education in the year in which we make the investment. It is an investment we make to be better prepared for whatever is next. Adopting an *above-the-line* view on strategy is not just about making the numbers today, but about making the choices that allow us to create value for all stakeholders for years to come.

> *'Society grows great when old men plant trees whose shade they know they shall never sit in.'*
>
> – GREEK PROVERB

THE WAY WE CREATE VALUE IS SHIFTING

How do we define success? It turns out that how we define success will have a significant impact on the culture we create and the systems we'll build to help us play the game of business.

Looking back at history, we find several examples of paradigms that we've adopted to help guide the way. One of the most significant ones, which has to a large extent shaped the form of capitalism as we know it, is Milton Friedman's theory of shareholder primacy. In his 1962 book *Capitalism and Freedom*, Friedman declared that 'there is one and only one social responsibility of business – to use its resources to engage in activities designed to increase its profits.' Friedman's proposal offered irresistible clarity for managers who needed to balance the claims of a multitude of stakeholders. They needed only to focus on making profits and the rest would take care of itself.

The pursuit of growth, a paradigm that we have adopted for the last couple of decades, has led to unprecedented levels of prosperity. Today, Global GDP is ten times bigger than it was in the 1950s. In just a few decades, we have shifted from a world of scarcity to a world of abundance. But while it is a paradigm that has led to abundance and extraordinary levels of wealth, it also has its shadow side – corporate greed, over-consumption and reckless exploitation of natural resources are just a few examples.

What we want to explore in our simulated world is how some of these systems assumptions are relevant to us and our business. Is the pursuit of growth the right approach for us? Should it be a measure of success? From a systems perspective, this is a very important question. Systems theorist Donella H. Meadows argues that 'systems run into trouble when they hold incorrect goals or paradigms. These are the deepest beliefs on which a system is built – like "growth is good" or "one can own land". If a system's paradigms are incorrect, they've got to be changed.'

We want to explore what kind of alternatives might be available to us. If we are free to make those 'how to play' choices, what paradigm will we adopt?

Friedman's idea may have once offered 'irresistible clarity' to managers. However, when we operate *above the line* on the strategy dimension of our *alignment & evolution* model, we have to accept that we will never find such irresistible clarity or be able to adopt a one-size-fits-all approach. Remember that complex systems are dynamic, self-organising, adaptive and counterintuitive. We can't afford to simply follow; we need to adopt the paradigms that are right for us. We need to select and monitor the metrics that are right for the environment we are in.

One of the most interesting alternatives to the growth paradigm that I have come across is Kate Raworth's book *Doughnut Economics* and her TED Talk of the same name. Raworth offers an alternative economic paradigm, with suggestions for metrics based on ensuring a basic social foundation (ensuring we aren't falling short on life's essentials – health care, education, housing, political voice) and a bounded ecological ceiling (the amount of pressure the planet can cope with – climate breakdown, ocean acidification, ozone hole). Raworth offers an insightful perspective on how we might thrive in the dynamic balance between the two.

But these are big social and economic issues. The conventional wisdom might argue that these issues are not the concern of business. Surely, business should focus on the money and let taxes and charitable donations help fund social issues? But when it comes to societal issues, business strategy expert Michael Porter argues, 'We're not making fast enough progress. We're not winning.' The solutions we are achieving on societal issues are small solutions; we are not making a large-scale impact.

In the *Ownership Mindset* chapter, we said that the purpose of business is to create value. This core truth has not changed. But as customers, our perception of value looks vastly different in a world of abundance than it does in a world of scarcity. Remember the box of matches metaphor? Very valuable in the wilderness; less so in urban life. Our perception of value is not centred around product, but rather around the problem the product helps us solve.

We create value when we solve problems.

And it seems like there is no shortage of those. Even before the world got shaken by COVID-19, the Edelman Trust Barometer (2020) gave us insight into the mood of our time: there is a growing sense of inequity; capitalism is failing; we worry about the future of work; we're unprepared for challenges on climate change.

'Consumers expect brands to act... customers will vote with their wallets.'

- 2020 EDELMAN TRUST BAROMETER

In a marketplace of sameness in which brands are struggling to find opportunities for differentiation, contributing to solving societal problems seems like the perfect opportunity to stand out. The most innovative and adaptive companies are doing just that. There is growing evidence that companies that are finding innovative ways of being regenerative and distributive by design are also extremely successful.

In her 'Doughnut Economics' TED Talk, Kate Raworth argues that 'corporations that still pursue maximum rate of return for their share-holders suddenly look rather out of date next to social enterprises that are designed to generate multiple forms of value and share it with those throughout their networks.'

The *ME* and *WE* games that we explored in the previous chapters were primarily about ensuring we could take care of ourselves, our teams and parts of the community. A successful *US* game is about taking care of all these stakeholders and simultaneously aspiring to turn the world into a better place than we found it.

In a world of scarcity, we contribute to society by creating high-quality products at low cost.

In a world of abundance, customers care less about what we are making and more about who we are being.

We need to practise playing *above the line* on the strategy dimension of our *alignment & evolution* model. To operate effectively in this space, we need to explore the following three themes:

- **Ethics & trust** – Alleviating widespread fears about the future.
- **Solving societal problems** – Understanding customers' perception of value in a world of abundance.
- **Strategic foresight** – Our ability to sense, shape and adapt to what happens in the years ahead.

OUR FICTITIOUS COMPANY IN CRISIS

We are more innovative and adaptive in situations in which we have no other choice. OzSwell is an opportunity for us to step into a crisis scenario. The longstanding recipe for success is no longer working. Reinvention is the only way forward. How will we challenge the rules of the game?

ETHICS & TRUST

The 2020 Edelman Trust Barometer claims that trust is built on competence and ethics. Based on their findings, ethics is three times more important to company trust than competence. What that means is that, as consumers, we expect companies to be good at what they do. But integrity, purpose and dependability drive seventy-six per cent of the trust capital.

So, how do we know whether we are being ethical in our decision making? Is it enough to subscribe to our organisation's shared values? Is it enough to have a just cause?

Having a clear set of values, or a well-articulated cause, is important, but it's not sufficient. Business theorist Chris Argyris differentiates between people's 'espoused theories' and their 'theories-in-use'. Espoused theories are the worldviews that people believe their behaviour is based on. Their 'theories-in-use' are the worldviews and values implied by their behaviour. They are the subconscious mental models we use to take action.

When faced with difficult decisions, we will subconsciously design action strategies that advocate our views, making evaluations and attributions in ways that ensure we are in control. Simulation scenarios allow us to test and uncover some of these subconscious mental models. How will we respond when faced with a difficult choice? Our 'theories-in-use' can sometimes be in conflict with our 'espoused theories'. It's not that we choose to make unethical decisions. We make decisions because we seek to be in control; we want to avoid feeling vulnerable or incompetent.

In the real world, we are under incredible pressure to deliver immediate results for a variety of stakeholders (e.g. our boss). And every stakeholder will always be interested in the metrics that support their immediate interest. We easily succumb to this pressure; staying true to the values is often difficult and fraught with danger (i.e. a career-limiting move). Our simulation environment gives us a risk-free space in which to test, uncover and learn about the unconscious assumptions we make.

SOLVING SOCIETAL PROBLEMS

To remain relevant, we need to bring novel ideas to the market fast. How are the decisions we are making today impacting not just customers but society as a whole, and why does it matter?

The UN Sustainable Development Goals (SDGs) – a list of seventeen global goals (see below) – might be a good starting point to help us evaluate our societal contribution for OzSwell, our simulated business. Do our current operations positively or negatively impact any of these items? What are the opportunities for making a difference?

THE UN SUSTAINABLE DEVELOPMENT GOALS

1. No poverty
2. Zero hunger
3. Good health and well-being
4. Quality education
5. Gender equality
6. Clean water and sanitation
7. Affordable and clean energy
8. Decent work and economic growth
9. Industry innovation and infrastructure
10. Reduced inequalities
11. Sustainable cities and communities

12. Responsible consumption and production
13. Climate action
14. Life below water
15. Life on land
16. Peace, justice and strong institutions
17. Partnerships for the goals

Let me share two real-world examples, for the sake of illustration.

In the last decade, innovations from companies like Tesla have changed the way we think about *affordable and clean energy* (goal 7 of the SDGs). Making the electric car a viable alternative has allowed us to imagine a future in which we as individuals can have an impact on (goal 13) *climate action*.

Innovative business models such as the Khan Academy have changed the way we think about (goal 4) *quality education*. Through its website, the Khan Academy aims to provide a personalised learning experience built on videos that are hosted on YouTube. It is not only changing the way we learn; it is making education accessible to millions of people who were previous poorly served or completely excluded from any formal education system. The flow-on effect may have a significant impact on other goals such as *reduced inequalities* (goal 10).

What these innovations have in common is that they begin with an innate understanding of some of the challenges society and communities are facing, for which incumbent players or current business models have not managed to find adequate solutions. It is undeniable that finding innovative ways to solve problems is winning stakeholder sentiment. On July 1st 2020, Bloomberg published an article with the headline 'Tesla Overtakes Toyota as the World's

Most Valuable Automaker'. This headline reflects perceived value, not sales. Tesla's manufacturing capacity is still tiny in comparison – their first quarter production was only four per cent that of Toyota. In this example, perceived value is not driven by Tesla's output, but rather by its mission – *to accelerate the world's transition to sustainable energy*. In just a few years, Tesla has changed the rules of the game for an entire industry.

The *Reinventing Organisations* simulation gives us a risk-free platform that allows us to take a completely different lens to value creation. It allows us to track and monitor the impact of our decisions on a wide variety of metrics and monitor both the short-term and long-term impact of our decisions. In the real world, it is not always possible to get the same kind of feedback. It might take years for the long-term, system-wide consequences of our decisions to play out.

STRATEGIC FORESIGHT

When we are confronted with an unexpected event, we have no choice but to focus on surviving immediate threats. In such circumstances, it is unsurprising when we make decisions that favour the present at the expense of the future. But if the decisions we make today have ramifications for years to come, we need to ensure we can do both – cope today and make the choices that prepare us for whatever the future brings.

Traditionally, we learn from past experiences. But in an unpredictable world, we do not have any historical reference points. To prepare for the uncertain, we need to use our current reference points to develop a range of possible futures. What are some of the environmental forces at play that could have a significant impact on our business or industry? Our simulation experience asks us to take a long view, and to imagine a reality several years from now.

By integrating scenario-planning experiences into our simulation, we get to learn from imagined futures. It allows us to work backwards to help us determine the actions we should take today. Through a process of iteration, we get to sense, shape and adapt to our future worlds. We get to develop our strategic foresight.

FINDING NEW WAYS

No one knows what the future will look like, but the world of business simulation gives us the opportunity to practise our responses to unexpected events and future-focused scenarios. Our simulation allows us to challenge existing beliefs, uncover biases and find new ways. It gives us a space in which we can explore 'what if' questions and new avenues of value creation. Rather than making guesses about what the future will bring, the simulation gives us an opportunity to start testing our strategies against a variety of possible futures. It allows us to be a step ahead.

FIND OUT MORE

The *OzSwell Simulation* is a great tool to help senior leaders discuss and consider current strategic choices against plausible future scenarios. It allows learners to step away from the pressures of short-term demands and consider strategic choices from a future-focused perspective.

Originally, this simulation was built mainly to deal with sustainability and ethics scenarios, and it was first known as the sustainability simulation. Since then, it has been modified to include several strategy-centric decisions and scenario-planning exercises. It is a leverageable platform, but the storyline, decisions and scenarios should be customised to be aligned with *your* business and *your* strategy. The *Connect with Me* section offers some additional ideas for possible next steps.

MESSAGE – FINAL THOUGHTS

All simulations are an abstraction of reality. That means it is less about creating a replica of your business and more about ensuring the challenges that learners engage with are relevant to them and their area of influence.

By practising responses to relevant challenges, individuals get to develop the skillsets that they need to make great decisions.

This section was about sharing examples in which the storyline was anchored in the business challenge we discussed in Chapter 2 – *the need to evolve to meet the needs of a fast-paced and uncertain environment*. We explored this challenge from three different lenses. Depending on people's roles and their level of influence, we adjusted the perspective, tailored the challenges and focused on skillsets that would be most beneficial for each audience.

Creating a custom simulation for your teams begins with *your* strategy and *your* message. But you do not need to reinvent the wheel. Where appropriate, you might be able to begin your customisation efforts by leveraging a simulation platform that can be modified – one which is fit for purpose.

PART 3

MEANING

SIMULATIONS ALLOW US TO GRAB PEOPLE'S ATTENTION. THEY allow us to experiment with real-world business challenges in a risk-free environment. But what does that mean for our day-to-day lives? How does that impact the performance of our organisations?

To get the full value out of any business simulation experience, it is critical that we can connect the simulation's key concepts to our everyday reality.

> *'Knowing is not enough, we must apply. Willing is not enough, we must do!'*
>
> – BRUCE LEE

The simulation narrative is born out of the challenges we experience in the real world. To make it easier to wrap our heads around these complex challenges, simulations allow us to simplify our world. We get to strip out the noise so we can focus on a few core concepts.

These concepts are the foundation of our simulation narrative. Our risk-free environment allows us to play lightly with these concepts and learn through discovery. But there is one more step, and that is critical. If we are not able to make the connection between what we experience in the simulated world and our day-to-day reality, the experience will not result in behaviour change. We need to be able to make meaning.

CRITICAL
CONNECTIONS

A FEW MONTHS AGO, I WAS DEVELOPING A NEW STRATEGY simulation for a corporate client. As part of the development process, I was interviewing several senior leaders to get a better understanding of the challenges their teams were facing. One of those interviews was with Mikayla, a senior HR leader. I was looking forward to speaking with her, since she had also been a participant in a business simulation workshop that I had facilitated several months earlier.

I remembered how engaged she and her team had been throughout the workshop. However, I had no idea how she might have applied the learning to her day-to-day work. When she shared her personal experience during the interview, I was blown away.

The actions she had taken following the simulation experience were remarkable. She shared examples of how she and her team had worked together on strategic projects to set up her division for long-term success. The simulation experience allowed her to develop a big-picture view which she was able to easily translate for her team. She was able to clearly articulate how their projects connected to the corporate strategy. They had clarity on how these projects contributed to innovation and value creation. She was more aware of the tensions and trade-offs they would encounter along the way and was able to share those with the team, thereby, ensuring everyone was on board.

She shared how the team dynamic during the simulation made her reflect on her own leadership style, recognising the need to be better at listening and considering other points of view. And as she continued to share details of what the experience had meant to her, it made me question whether a simulation experience was capable of such a significant transformation.

It made me realise one thing – it was not about the simulation. It was about Mikayla. She was able to take the concepts that were shared as part of the simulation experience and make meaning that was applicable just for herself. Only she could make those connections. The meaning she had made and the actions she had taken were uniquely hers.

When I interviewed her colleague Steve, I got to see a different perspective. He told me about a simulation experience that was part of his MBA program. In it, they got to play the role of CEO of a manufacturing organisation. He said it was a lot of fun! Then he bragged about how he had somehow managed to figure out the algorithm, make all the right decisions and win the game by a massive margin. I was pleased that Steve had a fond memory of the experience, but also acutely aware that, for Steve, the experience had lacked one of the most important elements. He had not been able to make meaning.

Steve's example is not uncommon. Not all business simulations are good or relevant. Just like not all business books are good or relevant. Building simulations is a form of authoring. We want to pick good stories that are relevant to the context in which we lead.

The experience needs to be relevant to where learners are on their personal leadership journey. If it is too far removed from participants' day-to-day reality, it will be difficult to give meaning to the concepts. The experience may be fun, and even insightful, but it will not lead to behavioural change.

IT'S A STORY, ABOUT US

There is a certain magic to simulation experiences that goes beyond anything we can intentionally design into the learning content.

The most powerful learning occurs in the individual who makes the link between the simulation experience and their day-to-day reality.

When we immerse ourselves in a simulation experience, we get to play in a conceptual world. The *Coffee Shop Simulation* is not about learning how to run a coffee shop. The coffee shop is a metaphor for taking complete ownership of a venture or problem. Just like the founders of your organisation would have been experimenting, exploring and making mistakes when the business was still in its start-up phase, so can participants learn from their mistakes in a simulated world that mimics the start-up challenges.

As learners, we can translate the experience of starting a coffee shop to projects that are part of our everyday reality. In the same way we use metaphors to help us make sense of abstract concepts, simulations allow us to make meaning in a world that is too complex for us to fully comprehend.

We need to rise above the everyday and develop the capability to make meaning based on the ideas that truly matter. When we make meaning, we make the shift from conceptual ideas to our own reality. It is no longer about the simulation. This is our story, and it is all about us!

THE CRITICAL LINK

When we immerse ourselves in a business simulation experience, we want to ensure that what we learn is transferable and leverageable back in our everyday lives. We need to be able to make the connection between the abstract and the concrete.

Figure 6: The critical link

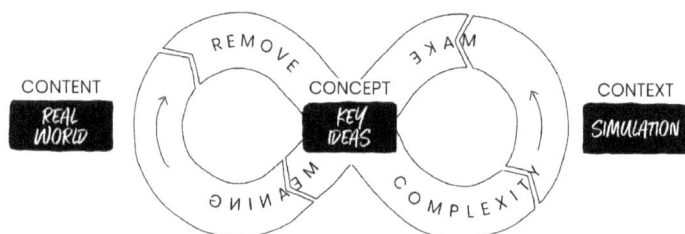

THE THREE DIMENSIONS OF AN IDEA

One of my friends and mentors is the founder of Thought Leaders, Matt Church, who explains in his book *THINK* that every idea exists across three levels of abstraction. These are:

- The *Content*, which is the stuff of life – the facts, the stories, the data, the financial reports;
- The *Concept,* which is the specific point we are trying to capture and share; and
- The *Context,* which is the abstract idea – the big-picture view often expressed as a model or a metaphor.

Let me briefly explain how these three dimensions relate to our world of simulations, and how they can help us make the link from the abstract and fictitious to the real and practical.

REMOVE COMPLEXITY

If I, the simulation designer, were to interview you and ask you about your business, you would share with me some of the *Content*. You'd be able to tell me stories about things that have happened, sharing facts, reports and data. You'd be able to tell me about relationships, the politics and the power plays. These stories and reports are full of complexity, more than I will be able to understand, even after a lengthy interview. And even for you, the organisation is full of unknowns. When I interview one of your peers, I will hear a different story, get a different perspective. In addition to that, I could add my own observations, based on books I've read, talks I've heard and case studies I've researched. In my hunt for information, I would eventually feel overwhelmed, realising that there is more knowledge available than I would ever be able to consume in a lifetime.

It is my job as the simulation author to translate that information into something that is digestible and easy to understand. To create a *Concept*, I need to strip away the complexity and be clear on the key ideas that I am trying to share. If the organisational objective is to push autonomy to the frontline (see Chapter 6), I might want to design a business simulation experience for frontline leaders that makes the following key points: we need a solid understanding of the business fundamentals; value creation is at the heart of what we do in business; and to be able to execute strategy successfully, we need to adopt an ownership mindset. Just three conceptual ideas that guide the entire experience.

Once I have clarity on the concepts, I create the *Context*. The *Context* is the abstract idea. It is the world of models and metaphors. These are simplifications of reality to help us better understand the landscape. Like a roadmap that allows us to get a big-picture view of our cities. This is the home of our business simulation – it exists in this contextual space. A simplification and abstraction of reality. Something that is easy to get our head around. Our coffee shop is a metaphor. It is close enough to our everyday lives that it doesn't require an extensive explanation. We have all visited a café before and can draw on powerful mental images and experiences. But what would it look like if we were to start our own?

Now the participant journey begins.

MAKE MEANING

As learners, we get to play in this contextual world. There are certain virtues to our virtual world that are extremely beneficial to our learning. We do not need to risk our savings or commit years of our life to take part in this learning adventure. We can take risks without having to be overly concerned about consequences. We get to experiment, adapt and try again. We get to learn from feedback in a short space of time. We're enriched by theoretical concepts and engaging discussions. Scenarios that uncover unconscious assumptions and challenge our beliefs. But there is more to it than that!

A simulation experience only becomes truly meaningful when we can connect the conceptual ideas back to our own reality. We need to be able to make meaning.

When designing the simulation, we removed complexity and narrowed down all the information we had gathered into a few core concepts. Making meaning – this final arrow on the infinity loop – is the same process in reverse. We give meaning to concepts by attaching our own unique personal stories, experiences and perspectives. And by doing so, we create something we can act upon.

Herein lies the difference between the simulation experience for Mikayla and Steve. Mikayla was able to close the loop. By attaching her own experiences to the concepts, Mikayla was able to make meaning, which she could act upon. She had gained a perspective that had allowed her to see things differently and was able to take meaningful action that was useful for her and her team. For Mikalya, the simulation experience led to behavioural change.

For Steve, on the other hand, the experience ended when the simulation workshop was over. They had played a game and won. It was an interesting and fun-filled experience, but Steve was not able to close the loop. Steve might have improved some of his technical competence, such as his financial know-how, but that alone will not drive behavioural change. The simulation experience was too far removed from Steve's reality to allow him to make meaning. And if we can't make meaning, it is difficult to take action.

Relevance is key! We cannot make meaning unless the concepts are relevant to where we are at on our journey as leaders.

If you run a business simulation for your leaders, obsess about relevance. We often put an extraordinary amount of effort into customising business simulations to look like our business. And I do not deny that there is value in customisation. But customisation based on problems is more important than customisation based on a specific business or industry.

Having a business simulation with a storyline that is not relevant to someone's current reality is like giving them a roadmap for the wrong city.

Our simulation will always be an abstraction of reality. There are many ways in which we can craft our storyboard, whether that looks like our own business or another. What we need to obsess about is that the *Concepts* are transferable and leverageable back in people's day-to-day lives. We want a platform that allows people to make meaning, to close the loop and make the learning journey complete. When we achieve this, behaviour change can happen, and a simple simulation experience can have a powerful impact on how people see the world and, more importantly, how they act in it.

ACCELERATE AND DISCOVER

Traditional training programs allow us to test and measure whether learners have retained the knowledge that was shared during the workshop. A business simulation isn't like that (at least, not the type of business simulations discussed in this book). The purpose of the business simulation is not to develop specialist knowledge, although there might be elements of that – the purpose of the business simulation is about understanding strategic choices in the context of the big picture.

We might strive for more autonomy on the frontline, but it would be nonsensical to expect new hires to be able to operate with autonomy from day one. What simulations allow us to do is accelerate the journey. We learn more quickly when we have opportunities to push ourselves beyond the levels of our current competence.

Our simulation experience allows us to go on a learning journey in which we can explore our world without the fear of failure and without the complexities and barriers of the real world. We get to play, explore and discover. We compete against rivals, make mistakes and learn from feedback. We gather insights and try again. We iterate and play until our simulation exercise ends.

The rest of the journey is uniquely ours – we need to make meaning and take action.

MEANING – FINAL THOUGHTS

We put an extraordinary amount of work into creating business simulation experiences that are fun and engaging. But if fun and engagement is all that they deliver, then there are simpler ways to achieve that goal.

The difference between a great simulation experience and one that is simply fun is this – our ability to make meaning. This needs to be what we strive for when we decide to invest in a simulation experience. Yes, it is a *game*, but I hope I have convinced you that there is a lot more to these learning events than just the *game* element.

The real value to you and your organisation is in this last part. This is where the magic happens – this is the part that allows people to make meaning and take action.

YOUR TURN

I HAVE SHARED SOME OF MY VIEWS ON STRATEGY EDUCATION and how we might leverage business simulations to help develop the skillsets we will need for the future. But a business simulation is about your business, your strategy and your people. No one-way conversation is going to give you all the answers that you need. I hope that this has been the start of a conversation that has helped ignite your imagination and that has sparked some ideas. I would love to hear more about your thoughts, your ideas and your challenges!

There are many approaches that you can take when it comes to simulation building. Perhaps you are keen to design your own. If you have the in-house capability to do so, that is the approach that I would recommend. If the complexity of the simulation solution you are looking for exceeds your in-house capabilities, you should partner with a provider you trust.

Whichever route you choose, it is important to keep in mind the objective of the simulation experience. It is not just about designing a flashy game – it's about delivering a powerful message, in a way that is engaging and relatable. That means we need to get the balance right between gameplay and a deep understanding of the business challenges our learners are likely to face, today or in the future. The magic is in the right combination of method and message.

The purpose of this book was to explain how the miracle of engaging learning experiences can change the way we see and engage with the world. I hope that it gave you some clarity on the benefits of simulations as a methodology for strategy education. That it gave you a sense of the types of skillsets a business simulation can help develop. Perhaps it sparked some ideas around possible simulation solutions for you and your target audience.

Ultimately, we create these learning experiences to ensure that our people have the skillsets to allow them to make great decisions in a turbulent world. Imagine the collective impact we can have when we realise the benefits of our strategy. When our people have a deep understanding of the challenges that lie ahead and understand how their actions influence the way forward.

As our world evolves and technological advances change what the future looks like, the challenge for business will look vastly different from how it has in the past. We will need to rise to this challenge, and our chance of success increases when we are better prepared.

We need to understand how we play in this complex world. A simulation experience can help us make sense of where the journey is going; it is a tool that can help us prepare for the journey ahead.

Let us go and take the first step...

CONNECT WITH ME

Thank you for picking up and reading this book. I hope these pages have provided you with answers to some of the questions you might have had about business simulations. And that they've sparked some ideas and allowed you to evaluate whether a business simulation is the right approach for capability development for your teams.

You can reach out to me via email or subscribe to my newsletter via simx-strategy.com. I would love to keep the conversation going.

Reach out to me to talk about business simulations in general or to find out more about demo sessions, webinars or the examples shared in this book. Or keep an eye out for public program announcements on social media and the simx-strategy.com website.

Here is some more detail on the simulation examples shared in Part 2:

- The **Coffee Shop Simulation** is a fully customisable simulation platform that can be run as a one-day or two-day face-to-face workshop or as a virtual session (usually over four to five sessions). Audience size for a simulation session is approximately twenty to twenty-five participants. The platform is usually customised for corporate clients, but this solution is also run as a public program with individuals or teams from different organisations.

- The **Secure-O-Tech Simulation** was initially created as a scenario simulation for conferences. Since then it has been run for audiences from as few as fifteen to up to two hundred participants. The platform has been built out to include a variety of operational decisions and can be run either as a two-day strategy-centric workshop (or virtual equivalent), or as a half-day scenario simulation for conferences. Customisation is recommended.

- The **OzSwell Simulation** was originally known as the sustainability simulation. It was built mainly to deal with sustainability and ethics scenarios. Since then it has been built out to include several strategy-centric decisions and scenario-planning exercises. It can be run as a half-day scenario simulation (recommended for conferences) or as a two-day workshop (or virtual delivery equivalent). Again, customisation is recommended.

I hope that someday we might be able to co-author or co-deliver amazing experiences for your teams! They are a lot of fun! The work gives me tremendous joy, and I look forward to keeping the conversation going.

Thank you!

Michael Schlosser

michael@simx-strategy.com
simx-stratgy.com

RESOURCES

INTRODUCTION

Senge, P. M. (2006) *The Fifth Discipline: The Art & Practice of The Learning Organisation*. Random House Business Books.

CHAPTER 1: THE CHALLENGE WITH LEARNING

Anderson, C. (2016) *TED Talks: The Official TED Guide to Public Speaking*. Headline Publishing Group

March, J. G. and Simon, H. A. (1993) *Organizations. 2nd ed.* USA: Blackwell Publishers.

Robinson, K. (2006) 'Do schools kill creativity?' TED Talks. www.ted.com

Sterman, J. D. (2000) *Business Dynamics. Systems Thinking and Modelling for a Complex World*. USA: McGraw-Hill Higher Education.

CHAPTER 2: THE CHALLENGE FOR BUSINESS

Bossidy & Charan (2011) *Execution: The Discipline of Getting Things Done*. Random House Business Books

Casserly, M. (2012) 'Majority of Americans Would Rather Fire their Boss than Get A Raise'. Forbes

Ford, H. and Crowther, S. (1922) *My Life and Work*. Garden City Publishing Company, Inc.

Harris, M. and Taylor, B. (2019) 'Don't let Metrics Undermine Your Business'. Harvard Business Review. www.hbr.org

Laloux, F. (2014) *Reinventing Organisations: A Guide to Creating Organisations Inspired by the Next Stage of Human Consciousness*. Nelson Parker

Q&A with Jimenez, J. & Sull, D. (2017) 'Bridging the Strategy Implementation Gap'. The Economist Intelligence Unit

Scott, D., Viguerie, S. P., Schwarz, E. I. and van Landeghem, J. (2016) *Corporate Longevity: Turbulence Ahead for Large Organisations*. Innosight. www.innosight.com

Taylor, F. W. (1911) *The Principles of Scientific Management*. Harper & Brothers

CHAPTER 3: CAPTURE ATTENTION

Hall, W. (2014) *Shift: Using Business Simulations and Serious Games*. William Hall

Obeng, E. (2012) 'Smart failure for a fast-changing world'. TED Talks. www.ted.com

Pine, J. B. and Gilmore, J. H. (1998) 'Welcome to the Experience Economy'. Harvard Business Review. www.hbr.org

CHAPTER 4: SHIFT PERSPECTIVE

Robinson, K. (2006) 'Do schools kill creativity?' TED Talks. www.ted.com

Schulman, T. (1989) *Dead Poets Society*. Touchstone Pictures

CHAPTER 5: RISK-FREE PRACTICE

CEB Inc/Gartner Research (2014) 'Reducing Risk Management's Organisational Drag'. CEB Marketing Research Team

Durso, J. (1968) 'Fearless Fosbury Flops to Glory'. The New York Times

Fratto, N. (2019) '3 ways to measure your adaptability – and how to improve it'. TED Talks. www.ted.com

Gates, B. (2015) 'The next outbreak? We're not ready'. TED Talks. www.ted.com

Gore, A. (2006) *An Inconvenient Truth*. Lawrence Bender Productions

CHAPTER 6: OWNERSHIP MINDSET

Butler, T. (2017) 'Hiring an Entrepreneurial Leader'. Harvard Business Review. www.hbr.org

Christensen, C. M., Hall, T., Dillon, K. and Duncan, D. S. (2016) 'Know Your Customers' "Jobs to Be Done"'. Harvard Business Review. www.hbr.org

Dweck, C. (2006) *Mindset: The New Psychology of Success*. Ballantine Books

Kim, W. C. & Mauborgne (2015) *Blue Ocean Strategy: How to Create Uncontested Market Space and Make the Competition Irrelevant*. Harvard Business Review Press

McChystal, S., Silverman, D., Collins, T. and Fussel, C. (2015) *Team of Teams. New Rules of Engagement for a Complex World*. Penguin

CHAPTER 7: TURNING STRATEGY INTO ACTION

Christensen, C. M., Hall, T., Dillon, K. and Duncan, D. S. (2016) 'Know Your Customers' "Jobs to Be Done"'. Harvard Business Review. www.hbr.org

Dignan, A. (2019) *Brave New Work*. Penguin Random House UK

Fried, J. and Heinemeier Hansson, D. (2010) *Rework*. Basecamp LLC

Meadows, D. (2008) *Thinking in Systems: A Primer*. Chelsea Green Publishing

Q&A with Jimenez, J. & Sull, D. (2017) *Bridging the Strategy Implementation Gap*. The Economist Intelligence Unit

Richardson, A. (2010) 'Understanding Customer Experience'. Harvard Business Review. www.hbr.org

Teixeira T. (2019) *Unlocking the Customer Value Chain: How Decoupling Drives Consumer Disruption*. Penguin Random House LLC.

CHAPTER 8: REINVENTING ORGANISATIONS

Argyris, C. (2002) *Double-Loop Learning, Teaching, and Research*. Academy of Management Learning and Education.

Argyris C. and Schön, D. (1978) *Organizational Learning: A Theory of Action Approach*. Reading, MA: Addison-Wesley.

Aziz, A. & Jones, B. (2018) *Good Is the New Cool: Market Like You Give a Damn*. Regan Arts

Carse, J. P. (2018) *Finite and Infinite Games*. Simon & Schuster Audio

Edelman, R. (2020) *Edelman Trust Barometer Report*. Edelman Intelligence. www.edelman.com

Raworth, K. (2017) *Doughnut Economics: Seven Ways to Think Like a 21st Century Economist.* Penguin Random House UK

Scobolic, J. P. (2020) 'Learning from the Future'. Harvard Business Review. www.hbr.org

Sinek, S. (2019) *The Infinite Game*. Penguin Random House UK

Stevenson, R. (2020) 'Tesla Overtakes Toyota as the World's Most Valuable Automaker'. Bloomberg L. P.

CHAPTER 9: CRITICAL CONNECTIONS

Church, M. & Cook, P. (2018) *Think: Using Pink Sheets to capture and expand your ideas*. Thought Leaders Publishing. www.pink-sheetprocess.com

ACKNOWLEDGEMENTS

I have been playing in the business simulation space for several years and am immensely grateful for the opportunities that have come with this type of work. I have co-created and co-facilitated simulation experiences with some amazing clients, and have had the privilege of sharing the stage with and learning about strategy from inspiring and influential leaders in various organisations. I have worked on some incredible projects with amazing colleagues who, many years later, continue to be some of my closest friends.

The opportunity to work on exciting projects with wonderful people has made it possible for me to write this book. Each simulation experience is shaped by the wisdom, experience, stories and passion of others and I have loved being part of the co-creation process.

I would like to thank everybody who has made this book possible. First and foremost, my family and especially my dad, who, as an author himself, has been the most encouraging supporter. I cherish all the long conversations we had during the writing process, which in themselves have made the hard work worthwhile.

My close friends, who have generously offered their time, their support and guidance – who have tested simulations, provided feedback on blogs and articles, and starred in promotional video clips – I am immensely grateful for your support. Your involvement in the simx journey brings great joy to my work.

To my team – Lisa for being the most wonderful supporter, for her uplifting energy and valuable advice. And Mark for his simulation support and wizardry when it comes to creating magical code.

To the members of the Thought Leaders Community for inspiration, encouragement and guidance. With an extra special thanks to my mentor Jaquie Scammel for being the best and most generous mentor anyone could ever hope for.

Everyone involved in the editing and production process. Kelly Irving for providing some incredibly valuable coaching advice and crucial feedback. Scott MacMillan, Sara Litchfield and the team at the Grammar Factory for making the editing and publishing process an easy and an enjoyable experience.

And finally, to the clients who have been champions for business simulations in their organisations. I am eternally grateful for the opportunities you have provided and your unwavering support of simulation experiences as a learning methodology.

ABOUT THE AUTHOR

Michael is passionate about creating immersive learning experiences that help teams develop the mindsets and ways of working that will allow them to thrive in uncertainty.

He has more than fifteen years' experience in the business and strategy simulation space, where he has worked as a simulation designer, author, speaker, facilitator and thought leader.

Michael has worked with global brands and several ASX 100 companies, such as ANZ, AGL Energy, Coles and Bupa, to support strategic alignment and strategy execution. He brings deep, industry-leading expertise to helping organisations execute strategy. He understands the importance of good strategy and is passionate about creating transformative learning experiences that are fun and bring strategy to life.

His programs are backed by deep research and offer practical tools that allow leaders to make a real impact in their area of influence.

Michael is German, grew up in South Africa and has been living in Melbourne since 2009. When he is not designing business simulations or delivering leadership programs, you'll find him at the beach, pursuing his passion for kitesurfing or playing beach volleyball.

simx-strategy.com

www.ingramcontent.com/pod-product-compliance
Lightning Source LLC
Chambersburg PA
CBHW071426210326
41597CB00020B/3671